100 DAYS

of

REAL FOOD

fast & fabulous

100 DAYS of REAL FOOD
fast & fabulous

THE EASY and DELICIOUS WAY to CUT OUT PROCESSED FOOD

LISA LEAKE

WM
WILLIAM MORROW
An Imprint of HarperCollinsPublishers

ALSO BY LISA LEAKE

100 DAYS OF REAL FOOD:
How We Did It, What We Learned, and
100 Easy, Wholesome Recipes
Your Family Will Love

100 DAYS OF REAL FOOD: FAST & FABULOUS. Copyright © 2016 by Lisa Leake. All rights reserved. Printed in the United States of America. No part of this book may be used or reproduced in any manner whatsoever without written permission except in the case of brief quotations embodied in critical articles and reviews. For information address HarperCollins Publishers, 195 Broadway, New York, NY 10007.

HarperCollins books may be purchased for educational, business, or sales promotional use. For information please e-mail the Special Markets Department at SPsales@harpercollins.com.

FIRST EDITION

Designed by Lucy Albanese
Food photography and styling by Lindsey Rose Johnson
Lifestyle photography by Daniel and Candice Lanning with The Beautiful Mess (with food styling by Cynthia Groseclose and prop styling by Carla Eustache with Style Perfect Events)

Library of Congress Cataloging-in-Publication Data has been applied for.

ISBN 978-0-06-243303-9

16 17 18 19 20   RRD   10 9 8 7 6 5 4 3 2 1

To my mom and dad,

for their unwavering love and support.

contents

introduction

> "After loads of extensive research and experimentation, I finally started to relearn how to food shop and cook for my family."

In 2010 I was given the wake-up call of my life when I watched an episode of *Oprah* featuring Michael Pollan, who was talking about where our food comes from, and realized that the Standard Amercan Diet we were eating might actually be a big problem. I went on to read his book *In Defense of Food* and learned that a lot of what I thought was healthy—and was feeding my family!—was actually highly processed, or what Pollan called "food-like substances."

I knew some serious changes were in order, but I struggled with where to begin. I literally lost sleep over what to feed my kids if goldfish and fruit snacks were no longer options. But I felt compelled to figure it out and dove in head-first. After loads of extensive research and experimentation, I finally started to relearn how to food shop and cook for my family.

It was hard to keep all these big changes to myself, so I started filling in family and friends whenever I had the chance—secretly wishing they would jump on board with us! Then one night I had an idea. What if our family of four took a pledge to go 100 straight days without eating any processed food at all? My hope was that our little experiment (which I documented and is still housed on my blog, 100daysofreal food.com) would help draw attention to how dependent Americans have become on processed food, show that a typical suburban family could survive (and even thrive!) on real food, and convince as many other people as possible to join us.

So, with my husband and kids (thankfully) on board, our journey began. I shared the details of our entire pledge online (and later created a budget version), with plenty of real-food recipes and shopping tips along the way. And little did I know how life-changing it would be. Slowly but surely my little blog grew from fifty readers (mostly family and friends) to millions around the globe, and in 2014 I released my first cookbook, which—much to my surprise—quickly became a national bestseller. My wish to spread this important message came true, and I'm thrilled you're here to join us no matter where you are on your own real-food journey.

WHAT'S IN THIS BOOK

The more I talk with my readers—from real-food newbies to those who have been on the bandwagon for years—the clearer it is that peo-ple are looking for fast, easy ways to integrate real food into their lives. And the truth is, it does not have to be complicated. My hope is that the resources in this book will help make this transition doable for you and your family. Change is hard at first, but simply take the first step and you'll likely agree there's no going back!

In this book you'll find 100 quick and easy recipes—75 of them new, never-before published—created with busy families in mind. But first you'll find the basics on how to identify real food and avoid the processed stuff, a list of my favorite grocery store finds and the super-market tricks I no longer fall for, and a new set of seasonal meal plans, along with some helpful food prep and storage charts.

supermarket staples and secrets

"Real food is made with five or fewer whole ingredients (or has no ingredient list at all)!"

Eating real food basically means avoiding anything highly processed. Sounds simple, right? Well, unfortunately the constant stream of buzzwords (thanks, processed food industry) and experts telling you what and what not to eat (thanks, diet trends) are enough to make your head spin.

After my huge wake-up call about processed food, I decided to completely overhaul my family's diet and learn how not to fall prey to those influences. In our new way of life, we aim to eat the traditional foods our ancestors survived on for centuries before us. This isn't a trendy diet—it's our new normal.

So, to help you get to *your* new normal, here are some cheat sheets that will show you how to identify real food. For a more in-depth explanation behind these choices, as well as the con-vincing reasons to avoid processed food plus even more wholesome recipes, take a look at my first *100 Days of Real Food* book if you haven't already.

REAL FOOD DEFINED: THE CHEAT SHEETS

What's the number one way to know what's in your food and how highly processed it is? Read the ingredient label (not to be confused with the nutrition facts label)! I like to aim for five or fewer *whole* ingredients, but identifying those whole ingredients isn't always as simple as it should be, so here are some cheat sheets to use as a guide. Take pictures of these charts with your phone so you can reference them the next time you're at the grocery store.

OUR REAL-FOOD RULES

In case you're new to our story, these are the 100 Days of Real Food rules we followed during our 2010 pledge to avoid all highly processed food, whether we were at home, out to dinner, traveling, or at a friend's house:

1. No refined grains; only 100 percent whole grain

2. No refined or artificial sweeteners; only honey and pure maple syrup in moderation

3. Nothing out of a package that contains more than five ingredients

4. No factory-farmed meat; only locally raised meat products

5. No deep-fried foods

6. No fast food

7. Beverages to include only water, milk, occasional all-natural juices, naturally sweetened coffee and tea, and (to help the adults keep their sanity) wine and beer in moderation!

WHY EAT THIS WAY?

I've always been up front that it takes more time and effort to put a wholesome real-food meal on the table than it does to pop a Hot Pocket in the microwave. But as we quickly learned, it's worth the effort for the health of our family. I initially overhauled our diets because I thought it was the right thing to do, but I was delighted when we experienced these unexpected changes in our health as a result:

- Improvement in asthma symptoms (i.e., less wheezing)

- Fewer overall illnesses

- Change in palate/less picky eating

- Constipation gone

For the adults:

- Weight loss

- Increase in HDL (good) cholesterol

- More energy

These were only the most obvious changes—so I have to wonder what other underlying long-term health benefits have been going on in our bodies. Regardless, it makes sense to know where your food comes from!

"It's worth the effort for the health of our family."

COMMON GRAINS

Look for	Avoid
Whole grains such as: • Whole wheat: flour, pastry flour, pasta (made from whole durum wheat), couscous, crackers, bread, and so on • Brown or other colored rice, whole-grain wild rice (usually a mix of brown and black) • Oats: rolled, steel-cut, and quick-cooking • Quinoa • Whole corn: flour/meal, masa harina, and popcorn	**Refined, enriched, fortified grains such as:** • Wheat flour (without the word "whole") and enriched flour found in a wide variety of products including crackers, bread, snack foods, cereals, couscous, baked goods, and so on • Rice (without the word "brown"), white rice, and enriched rice • Refined corn meal/flour • Semolina flour (often used in regular pasta) • Cornstarch • Most grits (unless made from whole corn) • Oat bran

DAIRY PRODUCTS

Look for	Avoid
Milk, cream, cheese, yogurt, and so on that is: • Organic • Plain • Whole-milk • Unsweetened • rBGH-free and rBST-free • Nonhomogenized (milk) • Pastured/grass-fed (see page 25)	• Low-fat and fat-free • Added flavors and sweeteners • Preshredded cheese (which includes anticaking additives made from wood pulp, i.e., cellulose powder)

LOW-FAT EQUALS PROCESSED

Trust me, I used to be on the low-fat (and fat-free) bandwagon, so I was caught pretty off guard by this one myself. But the idea is to go back to the full-fat traditional foods that have been around for centuries. Once you trade your watered-down, fat-free milk for the *real* thing, you'll be glad you did. If you're concerned about making this change, simply consider reducing your overall consumption (which is what we did)! See more on page 25.

ADDED SWEETENERS

Look for	Avoid
Natural sweeteners—and use in moderation, of course! • Honey • Pure maple syrup 	**Refined sweeteners:** • Sugar: white, brown, raw, and powdered (confectioners) • (Brown) rice syrup • Agave nectar • Cane sugar/juice • Corn syrup/high-fructose corn syrup • Refined/processed stevia • Xylitol **Artificial sweeteners:** • NutraSweet,* Equal,* aspartame[†] • Splenda,* sucralose[†] • Sweet N Low,* Sugar Twin,* Necta Sweet,* saccharin[†] • Sunett,* Sweet One,* acesulfame K,[†] acesulfame Potassium[†] • Neotame[†]

* *Brand names*
† *Generic names (found on ingredient labels)*

NATURALLY OCCURRING SUGARS ARE A-OKAY

Note: Naturally occurring sugars, such as those found in whole fruits and dairy products, are real-food approved since they come packaged together with all the other good stuff nature offers us in these foods! You won't see them listed on an ingredient label since they aren't added sugar, but they will contribute toward the sugar count on the nutrition facts label. I'm looking forward to the day when added sugar is broken out as a separate line item because they simply are not the same thing.

"Naturally occurring sugars, such as those found in whole fruits and dairy products, are real-food approved since they come packaged together with all the other good stuff nature offers us in these foods!"

COMMON COOKING FATS

Look for	Avoid
Organic, unrefined (oils), cold-pressed (oils), and/or pastured (butter): • Butter • 100% pure extra virgin olive oil • Coconut oil • Pastured lard (yes, lard!) • Clarified butter/ghee • Avocado oil	**Refined oils, whether they are organic or not:** • Canola oil • Vegetable oil • Corn oil • Grapeseed oil • Margarine • Shortening • Hydrogenated and partially hydrogenated oils

Cooking temp	Real cooking fat	Good cold/raw	Good for sautéing	Good for baking	Good for deep frying
Low/medium	Butter	✓	✓	✓	
Low/medium	100% pure extra virgin olive oil	✓	✓		
Medium/high	Coconut oil		✓	✓	
Medium/high	Pastured lard* (yes, lard!)				✓
Medium/high	Clarified butter/ghee		✓		
Medium/high	Avocado oil*	✓	✓		✓

* Also good for making tortillas

NUTS/SEEDS

Look for	Avoid
Products without refined oils and unnecessary additives: • Raw or dry-roasted almonds, cashews, and pistachios • Raw or dry-roasted sunflower and pumpkin seeds • One-ingredient nut butters • One-ingredient tahini • One- or two-ingredient sunflower seed butter	• Nuts/seeds roasted in refined oils (see "avoid" in the oil chart opposite) • Nut/seed products with added sugar and other additives

MEAT

Look for	Avoid
• Pastured poultry • Grass-fed beef products (see page 25) • USDA organic or organically raised • Locally and humanely raised • No added hormones	• Factory-farmed, conventionally raised, and grain-fed animals

SEAFOOD

Look for	Avoid
• Wild-caught • From your continent • Bonus: sustainable (the free Monterey Bay Aquarium Seafood Watch app is a helpful resource)	• Farm-raised (unless you are familiar with the farm and approve of the practices) • Added colors (especially found in salmon)

CONDIMENTS/SAUCES/FLAVORS

Look for	Avoid
Products with five or fewer whole ingredients: • Vinegars: balsamic, red wine, white wine • Soy sauce (organic and reduced-sodium preferred) • Mustard: yellow or Dijon • Pure extracts, such as vanilla and peppermint • Herbs and spices • Salt and pepper	Products with added sweeteners or refined oils: • Ketchup (it contains sugar, so this is a "sometimes" food at our house!) • Store-bought mayo (unless it meets the five-ingredient-or-less rule and uses a recommended oil) • BBQ sauce (go for homemade with a natural sweetener, in moderation)

A NOTE ABOUT EGGS

I aim to buy our eggs from the farmers market, where I can find them both pastured (meaning the chickens have spent time in a green field, i.e., a pasture) and organic. You'll find lots of other terms on egg cartons, such as free-range, cage-free, and vegetarian-fed, which are insufficiently regulated and can be misleading. My first book contains a full listing of the definitions.

Look for	Avoid
Organic, unsweetened beverages:	**Flavored, sweetened beverages:**
• Water, sparkling water and coconut water	• Soda of any kind
• Unsweetened tea (cold or hot)	• Flavored juices and beverages with added sugar
• Wine and quality beer (in moderation—one serving a day for women and two for men)	• Beverages made with packets of powder
• One-ingredient juices (in moderation, 2 to 3 cups a week)	• Most sports drinks (unless they contain no added sweeteners or artificial ingredients)
• Naturally sweetened coffee (I personally love maple syrup mochas)	
• Milk (see page 11)	

"If you're not a fan of plain water, try squeezing some fresh citrus, such as lemon, lime, or grapefruit, into still or sparkling water to add flavor (naturally!)."

ORGANIC VS. CONVENTIONAL

In an effort to keep things simple, I didn't list organic, organic, organic on every single one of these categories, but it's recommended when possible! If you can't buy everything organic, I would try prioritizing meat and dairy, as well as the Dirty Dozen List[1] and high-risk GMO crops,[2] which can both easily be found online.

OTHER COMMON REAL-FOOD INGREDIENTS AND ADDITIVES

Look for	Avoid
Familiar ingredients you would cook with at home, such as: • Fruits and vegetables, onions and garlic, beans, olives, capers, coffee, unsweetened cocoa, baking soda, baking powder, and so on	**Ingredients you would not cook with at home, including*:** • Artificial colors: Blue 1, Blue 2, Green 3, Red 3, Red 40, Yellow 5, Yellow 6, FD&C Lakes, Citrus Red 2 • Artificial flavors • Other food additives: maltodextrin, BHT, MSG, azodicarbonamide, and more

* *There are unfortunately too many additives in our food system to list here (and way too many to remember once you get to the store), so this is the rule of thumb I like to follow. The Center for Science in the Public Interest does have a comprehensive listing ranked by safety level.[3]*

Really strict rules can be hard to follow and to maintain over time, so when our 100-day real-food pledge had ended, we mostly still followed these same general guidelines, making some exceptions when we were traveling or out and about.

* I've found so many uses for my kitchen shears, including cutting fresh herbs, jalapeños, lettuce and other greens, cooked noodles, green bean ends, pita bread, and even hot items in a pan that I wish I'd chopped up more!

MY MOST USED KITCHEN TOOLS AND SMALL APPLIANCES

The right equipment can help when it comes to transforming all of these ingredients into yummy food! Here are some of my favorites:

- Good-quality knives
- Durable cutting boards
- Kitchen shears*
- Stainless steel measuring cups (good for dry ingredients)
- Glass measuring cups with handles (good for wet ingredients)
- Stainless steel measuring spoons
- Mixing bowls in various sizes
- Slow cooker (I prefer the 6- or 7-quart size)
- High-quality pots and pans (they'll literally last a lifetime; I love All-Clad)
- Cast-iron skillet
- High-quality blender (my fave is Blendtec)
- Immersion blender
- Food processor
- Stand mixer
- Salad spinner (great for lettuce, greens, and herbs)
- Baking sheets / pans
- Tortilla press / warmer
- Mesh strainer (essential for homemade stock)

GROCERY STORE ILLUSIONS: DON'T BE FOOLED BY THESE MISLEADING TRICKS AND BUZZWORDS!

Avoiding highly processed food at the grocery store is sadly not as easy as it should be. Food marketers spend billions of dollars per year (*billions!*) trying to convince consumers to buy their products. Then throw in a crowded Saturday, a cranky toddler, or hunger pangs and it's just too hard not to fall for the misleading buzzwords out there—Freshly baked! Grass-fed! Multigrain! Vine-ripened!

I wish shopping for real food weren't so tricky, but hopefully these tips will make it easier for you to separate myth from fact at the supermarket. And since I don't want to leave you hanging only with what *not* to buy, on page 30 I'm also sharing my first-ever "Top 10" list of favorite real-food products from a variety of national chains. My first book contains a full, comprehensive list of my weekly grocery buys.

Vine-ripened tomatoes?
Oh, please.

If you think "vine-ripened" grocery store tomatoes are superior and worth the upcharge, chances are it's just because you like that particular variety better than the alternative. There are six recognized stages of tomato ripening. The vine-ripened variety are picked during the measly second stage, which is referred to as the "breakers" because it's when the very first "break" in color occurs from green to red.[4] So picture a tomato that is more than 90 percent green with the tiniest hint of red, pink, or even a tannish-yellowish color—that's the ripening you're paying a premium for at the supermarket!

Unfortunately, though, supermarket tomatoes—no matter the variety—are notoriously flavorless compared to their homegrown (or at least locally grown) counterparts. When they're picked during these early green stages, which is optimal timing for safe travel off the fields, they're usually then artificially ripened in a chamber with ethylene gas. Now a tomato plant that's still fully intact will naturally emit ethylene gas when it's time for the fruit to ripen, but as I've said before—you simply cannot recreate or duplicate nature. So you end up with a tomato that may look nice and red but is not exactly ripe when it comes to flavor.[5]

I honestly didn't even think I liked tomatoes until I tried a locally grown one. I now count down to tomato season every single year!

The truth about baby carrots

You may have heard that common rumor that baby carrots have been "soaked" in chlorine. According to a statement from Grimmway (maker of baby carrots), the carrots are actually just processed with *water* that contains a small amount of chlorine, similar to what comes out of your tap. The amount present on the carrots, which is 4 parts per million (ppm), is "well within the limits established by the FDA" for drinking water. Believe it or not, the government regulation for chlorine allowed in a swimming pool is actually *less* than what's allowed in public drinking water, which varies by region but is generally only 1 to 3 ppm![6]

Baby carrots are made from specific carrot varieties that are smaller in diameter than regular table carrots. The white color that you sometimes see on the outside of baby carrots is called "blush" and it's the evidence of dehydration, nothing a little water bath can't usually solve. This can also happen to regular peeled carrots that you don't eat right away. So there you have it—nothing to be afraid of when it comes to those handy little baby carrots!

Freshly baked bread? Sure,
but not freshly made!

The grocery store (and even Subway) sure does a good job making it seem like they're baking homemade bread fresh from scratch in their

bakery. I mean, you can smell the aroma and even see the workers carefully getting it out of their ovens with your own eyes! But, while they may be *baking* the bread, they are certainly not *making* the bread, and there's a big difference.

In most cases the bread dough for supermarkets is made in a central location (a "factory," if you will) with a mix of highly processed additives, including preservatives and dough conditioners—all ingredients you would *never* use to make your own bread from scratch at home. That "freshly baked" bread is really no different from the bagged stuff already on the shelves and the one way to know for sure is to, you guessed it, read the ingredient label!

Wheat versus whole wheat

Somewhere along the way our society has given "whole wheat" the nickname "wheat." This causes a lot of confusion because if you see the word "wheat" on a label without the word "whole" in front, it refers to refined white flour. White flour and whole wheat flour come from the same grain, but the "whole wheat" version has all three parts of the whole grain intact while the "wheat" version has been refined, with the most nutritious parts of the grain removed. So the next time you see a box of "wheat" crackers, don't be fooled into thinking they're made of whole wheat. Check the ingredient label to be sure.

Multigrain versus whole-grain

Multigrain simply means a combination of different grains, but it doesn't tell us if those grains are whole. While a variety of grains is good, it is even better if those grains are whole, so you still need to look for the correct whole-grain terms (see page 11).

The unregulated term "natural"

I used to think the term "natural" meant that no artificial ingredients were used in a product. Then I saw a canister of powdered "lemonade" that said "natural" twice on the front of the package, turned it around to read the ingredient list, and saw not one, not two, but *four* different artificial additives (and of course no actual lemon in sight). The word "natural" is currently unregulated, and therefore meaningless when you see it on packaging, so as usual—check the ingredient list for the real story.

Low-fat? No thank you!

I used to think that "low-fat" meant healthy, and when I first learned the whole low-fat campaign was pretty much bogus, I was absolutely shocked. For years I binged on everything from low-fat Snackwell's cookies to fat-free flavored yogurt. But when food manufacturers started taking the fat out of their products in response to the latest "healthy eating" trends, they had to do something to keep them palatable, so they started adding refined sugar (a much bigger concern) and other unwanted additives (such as hydrogenated oils and cornstarch) to make up for the loss of flavor. The result? A food that is more processed than it was to begin with. And as it turns out, dietary fat is not the health disaster we once thought it was—it's our insane consumption of sugar that we should be concerned about!

Grass-fed—but how much?

Oh, I like my beef products to be from grass-fed cows—don't get me wrong—but there's a big difference between 100 percent grass-fed and grass-fed up until the last ninety days before slaughter, at which point they're usually switched over to corn (an option commonly found in our area). According to Michael Pollan, "you are what you eat eats, too," which means the health of the animal directly impacts the nutritional value of its meat. What if you lived your whole life eating a perfectly healthy diet (which is exactly what grass is to cows), but then you let all hell break loose for the last few months and chose to subsist on McDonald's and cigarettes? How healthy would you be then? Things can unfortunately go downhill fast, so be sure to look for 100 percent grass-fed on the label or ask the farmer yourself how the animals were raised.

Sugar-free is not a good thing!

When a packaged food is labeled sugar-free, it usually means the real sugar has been replaced with an artificial sweetener. According to the Sugar Association, these artificial replacements are "chemically manufactured molecules—molecules that do not exist in nature," many of which only entered our food system as recently as a few decades ago.[7] Why would I feed my family a substance that's so new we are not sure how it could affect our health long-term? Although we do avoid refined sugar as much as possible, I'd rather eat the real thing than artificial sweeteners any day. There's a full list of artificial sweeteners by both generic and brand name on page 12.

The "0 grams trans fat" fib

Found in everything from highly processed breadcrumbs to coffee creamer to flavored oatmeal, trans fats are considered to be the worst type of fat in our food supply and are known to increase our risk of cardiovascular disease, the leading cause of death in both men and women in our country. In 2015 the United States government finally announced its plan to phase out the use of partially hydrogenated oils (where most trans fat comes from), but food companies have up to three years to comply, so you'll still find it on store shelves today.

Now, here's the tricky part. You'll never find the words "trans fats" on an ingredient label, because, as I mentioned, the main source is actually from partially hydrogenated oil. And even when a label says "no trans fats," it may not be totally true—"the Nutrition Facts label can state 0 grams of trans fat if the food product contains less than 0.5 grams of trans fat per serving."[8] If you eat a few servings of foods that contain 0.4 grams of trans fat per serving, it can add up fast. This unfortunate loophole gives us one more reason to read the ingredient label!

A superfood to lower blood pressure, prevent heart attacks, or combat cancer?

Most superfoods are *real* food, and that's a good start. But seriously, some of the latest claims are over the top. I get why the word "superfood" was coined—it's a nonscientific way to describe foods with high levels of vitamins and minerals—but the superfood trend, while not exactly bad, still has us focusing on specific nutrients versus simply enjoying a variety of real, whole, traditional foods. We are one of the few societies that obsesses over tracking vitamins, minerals, protein, calories, fat grams, and the like—and look where that's gotten us. Food is not meant to just be a delivery system of specific nutrients for optimal health—it's about so much more, including enjoyment, community, family, culture, and even expressing yourself!

You don't need more protein, I promise . . .

Eating a high-protein diet seems to be a concern of many, so of course food manufacturers have jumped in and produced many new products and powders with high-protein claims. But it's actually "rare for someone who is healthy and eating a varied diet to not get enough protein,"[9] according to the Centers for Disease Control and Prevention (CDC). I estimated how much protein I might get in a day, even eating vegetarian meals and not paying attention to my protein intake.

BREAKFAST

- Granola: 10 grams protein
- Milk: 4 grams protein
- Berries: 0.5 gram protein
- Latte/Mocha: 6 grams protein

LUNCH

- Refried beans: 13 grams protein
- Cheese and sour cream: 2 grams protein
- Melon: 1.5 grams protein

DINNER

- Whole wheat pizza: 12 grams protein
- Spinach salad with cheese and pecans: 5 grams protein

AFTER-DINNER TREAT

- Peanuts and dark chocolate: 2 grams protein

DAILY TOTAL: 56 GRAMS OF PROTEIN!

The recommendation is that an adult female should have 46 grams of protein a day, and I exceeded that without even trying. As I mentioned, we are one of the few countries that obsessively tracks and adds up numbers in the foods we eat, which can add anxiety without much benefit. Instead, listen to your body and simply eat a variety of whole foods (without overeating) and the rest will just fall into place.

Chicken raised without hormones? It's the law . . .

Hormones (or steroids, for that matter) are not even permitted in poultry, pork, and goat meat by law, so if you see this claim screaming at you on your pack of chicken breasts, the producer is just bragging about something they're required to do. If you can't buy humanely raised chicken directly from the farmer, organic is usually the next best option!

No high-fructose corn syrup?

This claim is a classic example of buzzword trickery. Food marketers are no dummies, and they know that high-fructose corn syrup (HFCS) has been demonized lately; so, in an effort to sell more (of course!), they are slowly removing HFCS from their products. But, since they're commonly replacing it with regular corn syrup or other processed sweeteners, in my book it's not a change significant enough to celebrate!

Gluten-free does not equal healthy (for everyone)

I recently saw our local newspaper praising a food company for now offering "better for you" gluten-free snacks and other healthy options. I would bet that some consumers are avoiding gluten even though they don't truly understand what it is (or why they're avoiding it, for that matter). This is the power of buzzwords and diet trends!

Gluten is the general name for the proteins in wheat (and some other grains) that help hold the food together like glue. Some people are allergic to gluten (such as those with celiac disease) or have a sensitivity to it, but that doesn't mean it should be eliminated from everybody's diet. If you feel better without gluten, then by all means avoid it, but there are plenty of highly processed gluten-free products out there (made from refined gluten-free grains and other additives), so it's not the health claim some might think.

"If you feel better without gluten, then by all means avoid it . . . but it's not the right choice for everyone!"

WHAT TO LOOK FOR IN CEREAL

If you're not willing to give up store-bought cereal, here are some tips to help you make a decent choice at the supermarket.

1. **Nothing artificial**
   If the cereal looks neon in color or contains artificial sweeteners (or flavors) on the ingredient label, then just move right along. This one is a non-negotiable for me!

2. **Whole grains**
   Look for cereals that are 100 percent whole grain, or at least contain more whole grains than refined grains (the ingredient that weighs the most is listed first on the ingredient label).

3. **Low or no sugar**
   Does the cereal contain added refined sugar (listed under a variety of names, such as cane juice, rice syrup, agave, corn syrup, and so on)? If so, how high is it on the ingredient list, and how many grams of sugar are listed on the nutrition label? I would recommend options with no more than 2 or 3 grams of added sugar per serving.

4. **Short list of ingredients**
   The longer the list of ingredients, the more (unwanted) additives a product likely contains. Shorter is better in most cases.

WHAT'S IN YOUR CEREAL?

Cereal (listed from least to highest amount of sugar)	Sugar per Serving	Contain Artificial Ingredients?	More Refined Grain Than Whole Grain?	Score
Barbara's Shredded Wheat	0 grams	N	N	best
Puffed Corn	0 grams	N	N	best
Cheerios	1 gram	N	N	better
Rice Chex	2 grams	N	N	better
Kix	3 grams	N	N	better
Rice Krispies	4 grams	N	Y	bad
Special K	4 grams	N	Y	bad
Wheat Chex	5 grams	N	N	better
Barbara's Puffins	5 grams	N	Y	bad
Total	5 grams	N	N	better
Life	6 grams	Y	N	bad
Honey Bunches of Oats	6 grams	Y	Y	really bad
Ezekiel*	8 grams*	N	N (sprouted)	better
Fruity Pebbles	9 grams	Y	Y	really bad
Corn Pops	9 grams	N	Y	bad
Honey Nut Cheerios	9 grams	N	N	bad
Lucky Charms	10 grams	Y	N	bad
Golden Grahams	10 grams	Y	N	bad
Frosted Flakes	10 grams	Y	Y	really bad
Cocoa Pebbles	10 grams	Y	Y	really bad
Froot Loops	10 grams	Y	indeterminable	really bad
Heartland Granola	13 grams	N	N	bad
Honey Smacks	15 grams	Y	Y	really bad

* Contains raisins with naturally occurring sugar (7+ grams per tablespoon)

Recommended Maximum Daily Allowance of Added Sugar

Children ⟶ 12 grams† (3 teaspoons)

Women ⟶ 24 grams (6 teaspoons)

Men ⟶ 36 grams (9 teaspoons)

† 4 grams sugar = 1 teaspoon

MY TOP 10 REAL-FOOD SUPERMARKET PRODUCT LISTS

Some of these stores may seem like health food meccas, but they still sell plenty of processed stuff, so you always have to be on the lookout. The products below are either a good deal or hard to find elsewhere.

TARGET

1. Organic dried fruit—Peeled Snacks and Little Duck Organics brands
2. GoGo Squeez organic applesauce pouches
3. LÄRABARS
4. Simply Balanced organic 100% apple juice boxes (most other organic brands have added sugar!)
5. King Arthur 100% whole-grain whole wheat flour
6. Simply Balanced organic spices
7. Simply Balanced organic "canned" beans (actually packaged in a box)
8. Simply Balanced organic frozen berries and fruit
9. Annie's organic whole wheat shells and white Cheddar macaroni and cheese
10. Uncle Bens Ready Rice natural whole-grain brown (already cooked)

EARTH FARE

1. Earth Fare whole wheat gnocchi-shaped (pasta) noodles
2. Annie's Organic whole wheat shells and white Cheddar macaroni and cheese
3. Lundberg mochi sweet organic (brown) rice cakes, lightly salted
4. Back to Nature woven wheat crackers
5. Whole wheat pastry flour (in the bulk bins)
6. Arrowhead Mills puffed corn cereal
7. Ian's whole wheat breadcrumbs
8. Organic peanut butter
9. Wild-caught fresh seafood
10. Bulk spices

WHOLE FOODS MARKET

1. Organic fresh produce (good selection)
2. Seafood (this is the only place I can find peeled/deveined/raw shrimp from the United States)
3. 365 whole wheat breadcrumbs
4. Streit's Zahas whole wheat Israeli (pearl) couscous
5. 365 woven wheats (baked crackers)
6. 365 organic oven-roasted turkey breast (sandwich meat without carrageenan)
7. Whole Foods Market organic traditional hummus
8. Whole Foods Market Old World pocket pita breads (whole wheat)
9. Ezekiel breads and tortillas (freezer section)
10. Frozen produce

TRADER JOE'S

1. Trader Joe's 100% whole wheat pita bread (in various sizes; they freeze well)
2. Trader Joe's organic (original) hummus
3. Trader Joe's organic virgin coconut oil
4. Trader Joe's organic plain whole-milk yogurt
5. Trader Joe's clover honey
6. Trader Joe's raw nuts and seeds
7. Trader Joe's espresso beans
8. LÄRABARS
9. Ak-mak crackers
10. Organic wine (various brands)

WALMART SUPERCENTER

1. Simple Creations organic ground beef (100% grass-fed)
2. Smucker's organic chunky natural peanut butter
3. Smucker's fruit and honey strawberry and triple berry spreads (jam)
4. Bob's Red Mill old-fashioned oats (gluten-free)
5. Great Value organic dried spices
6. Pacific organic vegetable broth (low-sodium)
7. Great Value brown rice (this really is a *great* value!)
8. King Arthur 100% whole wheat flour (also a Pillsbury whole wheat flour option)
9. Chosen Foods 100% pure avocado oil spray
10. Great Value organic whole milk

ALDI

1. SimplyNature organic lightly salted popcorn
2. Freeze-dried strawberries
3. Roasted and salted pistachios (and in-shell peanuts)
4. Raw nuts and seeds
5. SimplyNature organic wildflower honey
6. SimplyNature organic creamy peanut butter
7. SimplyNature organic premium marinara sauce
8. SimplyNature organic 100% whole wheat pasta
9. SimplyNature organic quinoa (regular and tri-color)
10. Fit & Active instant brown rice

COSTCO

1. Organic spinach, spring lettuce mix, and kale
2. Tru Roots organic quinoa
3. Organic frozen berries
4. Kirkland organic peanut butter
5. Go Raw sprouted pumpkin seeds
6. Kirkland 100% pure organic maple syrup
7. Nature Nate's raw unfiltered honey
8. Mayorga 100% organic Cuban coffee
9. Frozen wild sockeye salmon
10. Cox's raw peeled wild-caught shrimp (peeled? yes, please!)

PUBLIX

1. Ezekiel cereals and breads/tortillas (in frozen section)
2. St. Dalfour 100% fruit spreads (jam)
3. Ak-mak organic whole wheat crackers
4. Strauss free-raised grass-fed (100%) ground beef
5. Streit's whole wheat matzos (crackers)
6. Publix GreenWise organic tomato basil sauce (marinara)
7. Annie's organic whole wheat shells and white Cheddar macaroni and cheese
8. Applegate organic uncured beef hot dog (grass-fed)
9. GreenWise organic frozen berries and vegetables
10. Stonyfield organic whole-milk plain yogurt

KROGER

1. Fage Total 2% plain Greek yogurt with honey (we usually just buy organic whole-milk yogurt, but these are fun with the honey on the side—though we don't use it all)
2. Simple Truth organic frozen berries
3. Ezekiel breads, tortillas, and English muffins (freezer section)
4. Lundberg organic brown rice cakes
5. Simple Truth organic whole wheat pasta
6. Annie Chun's (Asian) brown rice noodles
7. Freedom Foods free oats (quick oats berry delight)
8. Ian's whole-grain breadcrumbs
9. Kroger whole wheat egg noodles (only store where I've seen these!)
10. Smucker's fruit and honey jam

WHEN IS HOMEMADE WORTH IT?

I feel as if I already spend enough time in the kitchen, so if I can find a decent store-bought real-food option for something, I don't always rush to make it myself from scratch. This is when I think homemade is worth it:

Make these	(vs.)	Buy these
Salad dressing (pages 267 and 268)		Yogurt (see page 11 with what to look for)
Whole wheat bread (unless you have a true made-from-scratch bakery nearby)		Whole-grain Crackers
Ice cream		Applesauce (although it *is* super easy to do, page 147)
Seasoning mixes such as taco, gravy (page 279), and ranch		Ketchup*
Chicken broth/stock		Mayonnaise*
Chocolate sauce		Dry-roasted nuts
Granola (page 65)		Peanut and other nut butters
Flour tortillas		Whole wheat pitas (I like Trader Joe's brand)
Oatmeal packets (page 284)		

* These are not technically "real food," but we do use them on occasion.

I'm on the fence about the following items—sometimes I buy them and sometimes I make them. I *can* usually find decent store-bought options, but sometimes the homemade route can be fun and worth the effort!

- Jam
- Pasta
- Pure vanilla extract
- Corn tortillas

- Marinara sauce
- Hummus (Trader Joe's organic is a good one)
- Whole wheat breadcrumbs (Ian's brand has a good option)

WHEN IS HOMEGROWN WORTH IT?

There's lots of supermarket talk in this chapter, but lets not forget the items we can source from our local farmers markets and home gardens! The quality and taste of local usually far exceeds what you can get at the supermarket. These are the top ten items that I definitely prefer to buy locally (or grow myself, if possible) . . .

1. Tomatoes (see page 23)
2. Eggs
3. Meat
4. Herbs (it's *much* cheaper to grow your own)
5. Lettuce and other greens
6. Asparagus
7. Berries (if they're organic)
8. Lima beans (I didn't think I liked these until I tried them fresh)
9. Carrots
10. Corn

Check out chapter 2 in my first book for some helpful shopping tips for the farmers market.

As you think about incorporating these tips into your shopping routine, remember that your real-food journey doesn't have to be all or nothing. Any small changes are better than none, so set some goals that are realistic for you and your family. You can jump right in and get started!

FOOD PREP IDEAS AND STORAGE

If after restocking at the grocery store, your pantry and fridge appear to have no "food," just ingredients, that means you're doing something right! I've long said that we don't eat this way because it's the most convenient thing to do. The extra effort is simply worth it for our health, and trust me, it gets easier with practice.

The key to making the real-food lifestyle work for a busy family is planning ahead. You *must* spend time (on the weekend or whatever day works best for you) planning out your biggest meals, writing out a grocery list, purchasing food, and—last but not least—doing a little bit of prep work to make the week flow smoothly. This section includes make-ahead food prep ideas so all those ingredients can (not so magically) be transformed into delicious real-food meals, as well as four seasonal meal plans to help you get started.

Pick three or four items from this list each week to prepare or cook in advance for when you're hungry in a hurry.

MAKE-AHEAD SUGGESTIONS—NO RECIPE NECESSARY!

Food Item	Storage Location / Notes	Duration
Cooked bacon	Refrigerator	2 to 3 days
Baked white or sweet potatoes	Refrigerator	3 to 4 days
Cooked chicken (or other meat)	Refrigerator	3 to 4 days
Diced in-season fruit (such as melon, pineapple, and/or berries)	Refrigerator	3 to 4 days
Hard-boiled eggs	Refrigerator / Keep in shell until just before eating.	4 to 5 days
Mashed potatoes	Refrigerator	3 to 4 days
Cooked quinoa	Refrigerator	3 to 4 days
Washed and sliced raw veggies (such as carrots, bell peppers, celery, and/or cucumbers)	Refrigerator / Submerge carrots and celery in water	3 to 4 days
Washed lettuce or other greens	Refrigerator	3 to 4 days
Cooked whole wheat couscous	Refrigerator	3 to 4 days
Cooked whole wheat noodles	Refrigerator	3 to 4 days

MAKE-AHEAD SUGGESTIONS—WITH A RECIPE

Food Item	Recommended Recipes	Storage Location / Notes	Duration
Chicken salad	Sour Cream and Onion (page 85) or Tarragon (page 103)	Refrigerator	2 to 3 days
Dips for veggies	Tzatziki Sauce (page 275) or Smoked Salmon (page 170)	Refrigerator	3 to 5 days (tzatziki) 2 to 3 days (salmon)
Egg dishes	Egg Salad with Bacon (page 112) or Sienna's Deviled Eggs (page 83)	Refrigerator	2 to 3 days
Granola	Small-Batch Shortcut Granola (page 65)	Pantry / In airtight container	1 to 2 weeks
Hummus	Black Bean (page 93) or Hummus Without Tahini (page 276)	Refrigerator	3 to 4 days
Jar salad	Layered with White Beans (page 115)	Refrigerator	2 to 3 days
Muffins	Whole Wheat Lemon Raspberry (page 162) or Corn (page 169)	Pantry or counter for 2 days / Then move to refrigerator	Up to 1 week
Oatmeal	DIY Oatmeal Packets (page 284)	Pantry	Up to 6 months
Oats	Our Favorite Overnight Oats (page 62)	Refrigerator	4 to 5 days
Pancakes	Applesauce Oatmeal Pancakes (page 69)	Refrigerator	4 to 5 days
Pasta salad	Chicken Thai (page 89), Caprese (page 95), or Tangy (page 101)	Refrigerator	3 to 5 days
Salad dressing	Citrus Vinaigrette (page 267) or Fresh Ranch (page 268)	Refrigerator	4 to 5 days (vinaigrette) 2 to 3 days (ranch)
Salad toppers	Croutons (page 271) or Parmesan Crisps (page 272)	Pantry / In airtight container	Croutons best if used within 1 day; Crisps 2 to 3 days

(continued on next page)

MAKE-AHEAD SUGGESTIONS—WITH A RECIPE *(continued)*

Food Item	Recommended Recipes	Storage Location / Notes	Duration
Sandwich spread (or dip)	Veggie Cream Cheese (page 81)	Refrigerator	3 to 4 days
Savory cakes	Easy Baked Falafel (page 172)	Refrigerator	3 to 4 days
Scones	Cinnamon Raisin (page 61)	Pantry or counter for 2 days / Then move to refrigerator	Up to 1 week
Side salad	Couscous and Tomato (page 97)	Refrigerator	4 to 5 days
Snack bars	Copycat Cashew Cookie "LÄRABAR" (page 166) or No-Bake Peanut Butter Oat Bars (page 158)	Refrigerator	Up to 1 week
Soups	See soups and stews (page 181)	Refrigerator Freezer	4 to 5 days Up to 6 months

"If your pantry and fridge appear to have no 'food,' just ingredients, that means you are doing something right!"

GENERAL PRODUCE STORAGE GUIDELINES

Whole Fruits and Veggies	Pantry (Room Temperature)	Refrigerator	Freezer
Apples	Until ripe	1 month	
Apricots	Until ripe	5 days	
Artichokes		5 to 7 days	
Asparagus		2 to 3 days	8 months
Avocados	Until ripe	5 days	
Bananas	Until ripe	5 days (fully ripe)	1 year (peeled)
Beets		2 weeks	
Peppers, bell or hot		1 to 2 weeks	
Berries	Until ripe	3 to 5 days	1 year
Broccoli		5 to 7 days	
Brussels sprouts		5 to 7 days	
Cabbage		1 to 2 weeks	
Carrots		2 weeks	
Cauliflower		1 week	
Celery		1 to 2 weeks	
Cherries	Until ripe	3 to 5 days	
Corn		3 to 5 days (in husks)	8 months (out of husks)
Cucumbers		1 week	
Eggplant		1 week	

(continued on next page)

Whole Fruits and Veggies	Pantry (Room Temperature)	Refrigerator	Freezer
Grapefruit	Until ripe	1 to 2 weeks	
Grapes	Until ripe	5 days	
Green Beans		3 to 5 days	8 months
Green Peas		3 to 5 days	8 months
Lemons	Until ripe	1 to 2 weeks	
Lettuce		5 to 7 days	
Lima beans		3 to 5 days	8 months
Limes	Until ripe	1 to 2 weeks	
Mango	Until ripe	2 to 3 days	
Melons	Until ripe	5 days	
Mushrooms		5 to 7 days	
Nectarines	Until ripe	5 days	
Onions	1 to 2 weeks	2 to 3 weeks	
Oranges	Until ripe	1 to 2 weeks	
Peaches	Until ripe	5 days	1 year
Pears	Until ripe	5 days	
Pineapple	Until ripe	5 to 7 days	1 year
Plums	Until ripe	5 days	
Radishes		2 weeks	
Rhubarb		3 to 5 days	

Whole Fruits and Veggies	Pantry (Room Temperature)	Refrigerator	Freezer
Snap beans		1 week	
Spinach		5 to 7 days	8 months
Squash, summer		3 to 5 days	
Squash, winter	1 week		
Sweet potatoes	1 to 2 months		
Tomatoes	1 week	(Don't put them in the fridge!)	
Turnips		2 weeks	
Watermelon	Until ripe	5 to 7 days	
White potatoes	1 to 2 months		

"Once you realize what's in processed food, it makes it easier to avoid it!"

—SYDNEY LEAKE, AGE 11

MEAL PLAN: WINTER

A seven-day real-food dinner plan for a family of four and coordinating shopping list

MENU

Sunday: Homemade Fish Sticks (page 206) with baked sweet potatoes and steamed green beans

Monday: Easy Slow Cooker Steak Chili (page 197, double the recipe) with Corn Muffins (page 169, double the recipe) and a side salad

Tuesday: Weeknight Mushroom and Kale Pasta (page 231)

Wednesday: Simple Roasted Pork Tenderloin (page 228), Brussels Sprouts with Bacon and Apple Juice (page 140), and whole-grain wild rice

Thursday: Leftover steak chili and corn muffins with Citrus Salad with Crispy Quinoa (page 108)

Friday: Real-Food Sloppy Joe's! (page 223) with Sydney's Roasted Potatoes (page 151) and Simple Salad Mix (page 125)

Saturday: Kale, Sausage, and White Bean Soup (page 191) with buttered whole-grain toast on the side

SHOPPING LIST

PRODUCE

2 oranges

2 lemons

1 lime

1 bunch fresh cilantro (optional garnish)

1 small bunch fresh rosemary

1 small bunch fresh thyme

2 large onions

1 bunch green onions

2 shallots

1 head garlic

4 sweet potatoes

1½ pounds small potatoes (such as fingerling or new potatoes)

1 pound green beans

2 avocados (need ripe by Monday and Thursday)

1 pound Brussels sprouts

1 head celery (need 1 stalk)

1 carrot

3 bunches kale

1 head Bibb lettuce

Two 5-ounce bags/boxes spring lettuce mix

DAIRY/EGGS

1 dozen or half-dozen eggs (need 5)

1 pound butter

1 small carton milk (need 1 cup)

One ½ pint heavy cream (need ¾ cup)

One 16-ounce container sour cream

1 small block Monterey Jack cheese (optional garnish)

1 block Parmesan cheese (need ⅔ cup grated)

MEAT/SEAFOOD

1 pound mild white fish (such as cod, flounder, or rockfish)

3 pounds stew beef, cut into 2-inch chunks

1 pound ground beef

1 to 1½ pounds pork tenderloin (not pork loin)

1 pound Italian sausage links

1 package bacon (need 2 slices)

FROZEN

One 10-ounce bag corn kernels

INTERIOR AISLES: DRY/CANNED/GRAINS

1 bag whole wheat buns

1 loaf whole wheat bread

1 canister/bag whole wheat breadcrumbs (need ¾ cup—or make your own from the bread)

1 bag whole wheat flour (need 1¾ cups)

1 bag finely ground cornmeal (need 1½ cups)

One 16-ounce bag whole wheat penne pasta

1 bag whole-grain wild rice

1 box quinoa (need ½ cup dry)

1 package dried mushrooms (need 1 ounce)

1 jar pickles or relish (need ¼ cup chopped)

Two 15-ounce cans kidney beans

Two 15-ounce cans white beans (such as cannellini)

Two 28-ounce cans diced tomatoes

One 15-ounce can plain tomato sauce

1 package pine nuts (need ⅓ cup)

Two 32-ounce cartons chicken broth/stock (need 6 cups)

1 bottle dry white wine (need ½ cup)

1 bottle apple juice (need ⅓ cup)

PANTRY CHECKLIST

Apple cider vinegar

Cayenne (red) pepper

Chili powder

Baking powder

Cinnamon

Cumin

Garlic powder

Garlic salt

Honey (need ¼ cup)

Mustard

Olive oil

Onion powder

Paprika

Pepper

Salt

MEAL PLAN: SPRING

A seven-day real-food dinner plan for a family of four and coordinating shopping list

MENU

Sunday: Small-Batch Shrimp Boil (page 232) with a side salad

Monday: Weeknight Beef Bourguignon (page 241) over whole-grain noodles and Made-from-Scratch Simple Gravy on top (page 279)

Tuesday: Cobb Salad (page 123)

Wednesday: White Chicken Chili (page 188) with a side salad

Thursday: Creamy Mac and Peas (page 209)

Friday: Slow Cooker Shredded Pork and Bean Tacos (page 238; use a 3- to 3½-pound roast for leftovers) with Lime and Cilantro Coleslaw (page 132) and whole-grain tortillas

Saturday: Taco Salad (page 91) using the leftover slow cooker shredded pork instead of a new ground beef mixture and the leftover coleslaw as the lettuce (or mixed with lettuce, depending on how much is left over)

SHOPPING LIST

PRODUCE

1 pear (ripe by Tuesday)

3 limes

2 bunches cilantro

3 onions

1 bunch green onions or chives (need ¼ cup
    chopped)

1 head garlic (need 2 cloves)

¾ pound red potatoes

1 or 2 jalapeños

3 ears corn

4 avocados (2 ripe by Tuesday, 1 Wednesday,
    and 1 Friday)

4 tomatoes (or equivalent in cherry tomatoes)

1 bag carrots (need 3 or 4)

1 head celery (need 3 or 4 stalks)

2 bags/boxes lettuce (for 2 salads of your choice)

1 head lettuce (any variety)

6 cups sliced cabbage mix (such as green and/or
    red cabbage and julienned carrots)

DAIRY/EGGS

1 dozen or half-dozen eggs (need 3)

1 pound butter (need ¼ stick)

1 pint heavy cream

One 16-ounce container sour cream

3 to 4 ounces blue cheese

One 8-ounce block Cheddar cheese (need
    2½ cups grated)

One 8-ounce block Monterey Jack cheese
    (need 2 cups grated)

MEAT/SEAFOOD

½ pound smoked sausage, any variety

One 3- to 3½-pound boneless pork shoulder
    or Boston butt roast

1 pound large shrimp

2½ pounds stew beef

2 packages bacon (need 12 to 13 slices)

1 pound boneless, skinless chicken breasts

FROZEN

One 10-ounce bag corn kernels

One 10-ounce bag peas

INTERIOR AISLES: DRY/CANNED/GRAINS

One 16-ounce bag whole-grain noodles

One 16-ounce bag whole wheat macaroni/elbow
    noodles

Two 12-packs whole-grain corn tortillas

Whole wheat flour

Two 32-ounce cartons chicken broth/stock

1 bottle dry red wine (need 2 cups)

Two 15-ounce cans white beans (such as
    Great Northern or cannellini)

Two 15-ounce cans black (or pinto) beans

Old Bay seasoning (need 2 tablespoons)

PANTRY CHECKLIST

Cayenne (red) pepper

Chili powder

Cumin

Dijon mustard

Dried thyme

Honey (need 2 teaspoons)

Olive oil

Oregano

Paprika

Pepper

Red wine vinegar

Salt

MEAL PLAN: SUMMER

A seven-day real-food dinner plan for a family of four and coordinating shopping list

MENU

Sunday: Easy Fish Tacos with Pico de Gallo (page 218) and shredded cabbage on top

Monday: Sausage and Pepper Frittata (page 73) with baked potatoes and a side salad

Tuesday: Roasted Summer Vegetable Pasta (page 220)

Wednesday: Parmesan-Crusted Chicken (page 217) with Couscous and Tomato Salad (page 97; double the recipe) and steamed green beans

Thursday: Coconut Shrimp (page 176) with Asian Rice Noodle Salad (page 116)

Friday: Lamb Burgers (page 215) in whole wheat pitas with Tzatziki Sauce (page 275), leftover couscous and tomato salad, and a side salad

Saturday: Black Bean Bowls (page 205) topped with avocado and diced tomatoes and grilled corn on the side

SHOPPING LIST

PRODUCE

2 large lemons (or 3 small)
4 limes
1 bunch cilantro
1 bunch parsley
1 bunch mint
1 bunch fresh dill (or use dried dill)
1 inch fresh ginger (need 1 teaspoon minced)
1 white onion
1 yellow onion
1 bunch green onions
1 shallot
1 head garlic
4 baking potatoes
4 ears corn
1 head, or ½ head if available, cabbage
    (for topping fish tacos)

2½ cups chopped cabbage mix (for coleslaw)
3 medium tomatoes (about ¾ pound total)
2 Roma tomatoes (optional)
1 pint cherry tomatoes
1 serrano or jalapeño pepper
1 red bell pepper
4 ounces mushrooms, any variety
1 eggplant, 12 to 13 ounces
2 medium zucchini (or other summer squash),
    7 to 8 ounces each
2 cucumbers
1 pound green beans
1 avocado (ripe for Saturday to top black bean
    bowls)
Two 5-ounce bags/boxes lettuce (for salad
    of choice)

DAIRY/EGGS

1 dozen eggs
1 pound butter (need 1 stick)
1 container plain yogurt (need 1½ cups)
1 small container sour cream (optional garnish)
1 block Parmesan cheese (need just under 1½ cups grated)
One 8-ounce package feta cheese (need 1 cup crumbled)

MEAT/SEAFOOD

2 links Italian sausage
1 pound white fish (such as cod, rockfish, or tilapia)
1 pound boneless, skinless chicken breasts
1 pound ground lamb

FROZEN

1 pound large shrimp (buy frozen and thaw for Thursday)

INTERIOR AISLES: DRY/CANNED/GRAINS

1 bag whole-grain corn or flour tortillas
1 bag whole wheat pita bread
1 package whole wheat breadcrumbs
One 16-ounce package whole-grain spaghetti or pasta
One 8-ounce box Asian brown rice (whole-grain) noodles
One 16-ounce package whole wheat couscous, Israeli (pearl) or regular (need 2 cups dry)
One 16-ounce bag brown rice (need 4 servings / 1 cup dry)
1 small bag whole wheat flour
1 bottle dry white wine
Two 15-ounce cans black beans
One 15-ounce can plain tomato sauce
1 jar pitted Greek olives (optional, but recommended)
One 8-ounce bag unsweetened shredded coconut
1 can salted dry-roasted peanuts or cashews (need ¾ cup chopped)

PANTRY CHECKLIST

Cayenne (red) pepper
Chili powder
Coconut oil (or butter)
Cumin
Dill
Honey
Olive oil
Pepper
Rice vinegar
Red wine vinegar
Salt
Soy sauce
Toasted sesame oil
Thyme

MEAL PLAN: FALL

A seven-day real-food dinner plan for a family of four and coordinating shopping list

MENU

Sunday: Simple Salmon with Pinot Noir (page 224) with Asparagus with Easy Dijon Sauce (page 136) and whole-grain wild rice

Monday: Layered Jar Salad with White Beans (page 115) and grilled sausages

Tuesday: Slow Cooker Black Bean Soup (page 192; double the recipe) with sour cream and diced bell peppers on top and Simple Skillet Cornbread (page 148)

Wednesday: Crispy Pork with a Cracker Crust (page 210) with Cheesy Hash Brown Casserole (page 66; double the recipe) and a spinach side salad

Thursday: Scrambled or fried eggs with leftover hash brown casserole and steamed broccoli

Friday: Taco Stuffed Peppers (page 235) with leftover black bean soup and brown rice

Saturday: Quick Cauliflower Soup (page 185) with grilled cheese on whole wheat bread and a spinach side salad

SHOPPING LIST

PRODUCE

1 lime
1 bunch thyme (optional garnish)
1 bunch basil
1 bunch cilantro
1 red onion
4 onions
1 shallot
1 head garlic
1 pound asparagus
1 pound broccoli
1 head cauliflower
6 bell peppers (any color)
2 jalapeños
1 tomato
One 5-ounce bag/box arugula
Two 5-ounce bags/boxes spinach
    (for 2 side salads)

DAIRY/EGGS

1 dozen eggs
1 pound butter
1 quart milk (need 3 cups)
8 ounces heavy cream
One 8- or 16-ounce container sour cream
1 small carton buttermilk (need 1½ cups)
1 block Parmesan cheese (need ½ cup grated)
Two 8-ounce blocks mild Cheddar cheese
    (need 4 cups grated)
One 8-ounce block Monterey Jack cheese
    (need 1 cup grated)

MEAT/SEAFOOD

1 pound wild-caught salmon
4 sausage links, any variety (for grilling)
4 boneless pork chops, about ¾ inch thick
1 pound ground pork or beef

FROZEN

2 pounds hash browns (should have only
    1 ingredient—potatoes)

INTERIOR AISLES: DRY/CANNED/GRAINS

1 loaf whole wheat bread
One 8-ounce box woven wheat crackers
    (such as Back to Nature or Triscuits)
One 24-ounce package fine ground cornmeal
    (need 2 cups)
One 16-ounce package whole-grain wild rice
    (need 4 servings / 1 cup dry)
One 16-ounce package brown rice (need
    4 servings / 1 cup dry)
One 2-pound package whole wheat flour
One 15-ounce can cannellini beans
1-pound bag dried black beans
1 small bottle lemon pepper seasoning
Three 32-ounce cartons chicken or vegetable broth
1 bottle Pinot Noir (need ½ cup)
One 4-ounce package walnuts (need ½ cup
    chopped)

PANTRY CHECKLIST

Baking powder
Baking soda
Balsamic vinegar
Chili powder
Cumin
Dijon mustard
Garlic powder
Nutmeg
Olive oil
Onion powder
Oregano
Paprika
Pepper
Salt
Thyme (dried)

FULL MEAL PLAN TEMPLATE

DAY	BREAKFAST	LUNCH	SNACK	DINNER
Sunday				
Monday				
Tuesday				
Wednesday				
Thursday				
Friday				
Saturday				

Recipes that should be made in advance over the weekend for the upcoming week:

Recipe 1:

Recipe 2:

Recipe 3:

SHOPPING LIST TEMPLATE

PRODUCE

Qty.	Item

INTERIOR AISLES:
DRY / CANNED / GRAINS

Qty.	Item

MEAT / SEAFOOD

Qty.	Item

FROZEN

Qty.	Item

BULK / MISC / OTHER

Qty.	Item

DAIRY / EGGS

Qty.	Item

PANTRY CHECKLIST (ITEMS YOU HAVE ON HAND)

Item	Item
☐	☐
☐	☐
☐	☐
☐	☐
☐	☐
☐	☐
☐	☐
☐	☐

breakfast

breakfast recipes

Avocado Toast

Smashed avocado on toast is all the rage for good reason. This super tasty version was inspired by a breakfast I had at California's Big Sur Bakery on our cross-country RV trip back in 2014. Part of what makes this recipe so good is the technique for toasting the bread in the pan. It's actually similar to how I make grilled cheese except without the cheese, which isn't as much of a travesty as it sounds.

1. In a sauté pan, melt the butter over medium-low heat. Add the bread and cook until toasted brown, 2 to 3 minutes per side. Set aside on a plate.

2. Halve the avocado and remove the pit. Scoop the flesh out into a medium bowl and mash with the back of a fork until smooth.

3. Add the parsley, green onions, lemon juice, olive oil, and salt (don't be shy) and mix thoroughly.

4. Spread the avocado mixture on the toasts. Top with the radish slices, garnish with more green onions, if desired, and serve.

> **LISA'S TIP:** One of my recipe testers said this dish opened her eyes to using radishes. If you're not generally a fan, give them a try here anyway—you might be surprised!

Difficulty: Easy

Prep time: Less than 10 minutes

Cook time: Less than 5 minutes

Seasonal note: Use locally grown parsley in the summer months and radishes in the spring.

Makes 3 or 4 side servings

GLUTEN-FREE (IF GLUTEN-FREE BREAD IS USED)

DAIRY-FREE (IF OLIVE OIL IS SUBSTITUTED FOR THE BUTTER)

VEGETARIAN

NUT-FREE

1 tablespoon butter

3 or 4 slices good-quality whole wheat bread (depending on how big your bread is!)

1 avocado

1 tablespoon chopped fresh parsley

1 tablespoon chopped green onions, white and green parts, plus extra for garnish

2 teaspoons fresh lemon juice

1 teaspoon olive oil

Salt

1 or 2 large or 3 small radishes, thinly sliced

Simple Yogurt Crunch

Difficulty: Easy
Prep time: Less than 5 minutes
Cook time: Less than 5 minutes
Makes 2 or 3 servings
Seasonal note: Use locally grown berries in the summer months.

GLUTEN-FREE
VEGETARIAN

2 cups plain yogurt (we prefer organic whole-milk yogurt)

4 teaspoons pure maple syrup or honey, divided

¼ teaspoon pure vanilla extract

1 tablespoon butter

1 cup sliced almonds and/or pecan halves

A few handfuls of mixed berries (frozen or fresh)

It's no secret that I love to start my day with a bowl of homemade granola, but with numerous ingredients involved and a whopping 75 minutes to bake, I just don't always have some on hand (especially when traveling). So I got a little creative and the result is even better than I expected—it's quickly become my second favorite breakfast!

1. In a medium bowl, mix together the yogurt, 2 teaspoons of the maple syrup or honey, and the vanilla. Divide between 2 or 3 cereal bowls and set aside.

2. In a medium sauté pan, melt the butter over medium heat. Add the nuts and stir until well coated. Drizzle the remaining 2 teaspoons maple syrup or honey over the top and cook until lightly toasted and browned, 1 to 2 minutes. Nuts can go from perfect to burned very quickly, so don't turn away! It's important to remove them from the pan as soon as they are ready.

3. Spoon equal amounts of the nut mixture into the yogurt bowls, toss a handful of berries on top, and serve.

Cinnamon Raisin Scones

When I told my eleven-year-old that scones were like a combination of biscuits and muffins, she could barely contain her excitement. She then went on to almost single-handedly deplete the entire first batch I had made—in the space of only twenty-four hours.

1. Preheat the oven to 400°F.

2. In the food processor fitted with a dough blade, process the flour, baking powder, cinnamon, and salt. Add the walnuts (if using) and raisins and pulse just until combined.

3. Cut the butter into tablespoon-size chunks and sprinkle them on top of the flour mixture. Pulse until you have a crumbly mixture. (If you don't have a food processor, you can do it by hand with a pastry blender.)

4. Add 2 of the eggs, the cream, and honey and process until the dough comes together into one ball chasing itself around the machine (or if it's still too sticky to form into a ball, you can just bring it together with your hands and add a little extra flour).

5. Turn the dough out onto a lightly floured surface, sprinkle the top with flour, and pat it down a little. Using your hands (or a rolling pin), form it into an 8-inch round about ¾ inch thick.

6. Cut the dough into wedges as you would a pizza and carefully transfer them to the ungreased baking sheet.

7. Whisk the last egg with a splash of water and brush this egg wash on top of the dough to help with browning.

8. Bake until golden brown, 12 to 15 minutes. Serve warm or at room temperature.

Difficulty: Medium
Prep time: Less than 20 minutes
Cook time: Less than 15 minutes
Makes about 1 dozen scones
Special tools needed: Food processor and baking sheet

VEGETARIAN
NUT-FREE (OMIT THE WALNUTS)
FREEZER-FRIENDLY

2 cups whole wheat flour or whole wheat pastry flour, plus more for rolling and shaping

1 tablespoon baking powder

1 tablespoon ground cinnamon

½ teaspoon salt

½ cup chopped walnuts (optional)

⅔ cup raisins

1 stick (4 ounces) cold butter (straight out of the fridge)

3 eggs, divided

½ cup heavy cream

3 tablespoons honey

Our Favorite Overnight Oats

Difficulty: Super easy

Prep time: 5 minutes

"Cook" time: 5 hours in the fridge

Makes 1 serving

Special tools needed: 8-ounce jar (or other container) with tight-fitting lid

GLUTEN-FREE (IF GLUTEN-FREE OATS ARE USED)
VEGETARIAN
NUT-FREE

½ cup rolled oats

½ cup milk

1 tablespoon plain yogurt

½ teaspoon honey

1 to 2 tablespoons raisins (depending on how much you like raisins!)

⅛ teaspoon pure vanilla extract

⅛ teaspoon ground cinnamon

The idea of overnight oats intrigued me for a long time, and then one day we finally tried them and have never looked back! My older daughter loves these anytime of day . . . breakfast, (as part of) lunch, or for a snack. So I like to make a batch on Sunday for her to just grab and go during the week.

Combine all the ingredients in the jar (or other storage container), cover, shake briefly to mix, and refrigerate for a minimum of 5 hours before eating.

LISA'S TIP: I usually make 4 to 6 jars at a time in an assembly-line fashion so they'll last throughout the week. A funnel (like those that come in canning kits) helps make the process quick and mess-free.

Small-Batch Shortcut Granola

Homemade granola is my most favorite breakfast of all time. So I'm excited to introduce this quick and easy alternative for the days when you didn't plan ahead by making the version that takes over an hour to bake.

1. Preheat the broiler to high. Line the baking sheet with parchment paper. (Note: I don't normally recommend parchment paper with the broiler, but this one is in the oven for such a short amount of time there are no issues.)

2. In a medium bowl, combine the oats, nut/seed mixture, and pumpkin pie spice. Melt the butter and honey together in a small saucepan on the stove (or in the microwave) and pour it over the oat mixture. Stir to combine.

3. Spread the mixture in an even layer on the prepared baking sheet. Place it on the bottom oven rack and broil for 1 minute. Stir, then broil for 1 minute more. Repeat until the granola is golden brown, 3 to 4 minutes total.

4. Let the granola cool, then eat it with milk or plain yogurt and fresh berries, if desired.

"A shortcut for my favorite breakfast!"

Difficulty: Easy

Prep time: 5 minutes

Cook time: 5 minutes

Makes 2 servings

Special tools needed: Rimmed baking sheet and parchment paper

GLUTEN-FREE (IF GLUTEN-FREE OATS ARE USED)
DAIRY-FREE (IF COCONUT OIL IS USED INSTEAD OF BUTTER)
VEGETARIAN

⅔ **cup rolled oats**

⅔ **cup mixed raw nuts and/or seeds (such as cashews, sliced almonds, pumpkin seeds, and sunflower seeds)**

½ **teaspoon pumpkin pie spice**

1 tablespoon butter

1 tablespoon honey

Milk, plain yogurt, and/or berries (optional), for serving

Cheesy Hash Brown Casserole

Difficulty: Medium

Prep time: 10 to 15 minutes

Cook time: 30 to 35 minutes
   (hands off)

Makes 5 or 6 servings

Special tools needed: 8- or
   9-inch square baking dish

VEGETARIAN
NUT-FREE

6 tablespoons butter, plus more
for greasing the baking dish

⅓ cup diced onion

1 garlic clove, minced

¼ cup whole wheat flour

1½ cups milk

½ teaspoon salt

Ground black pepper

2 cups freshly grated mild
Cheddar cheese

1 pound frozen hash browns,
no need to thaw (be sure to buy
a brand with only 1 ingredient:
potatoes!)

> **LISA'S TIP:** This rec-
> ipe works best with fro-
> zen hash browns—not
> fresh! And believe me,
> I've tried.

I used to love the hash brown casserole at Cracker Barrel. That's before I started asking questions about how restaurants make their food. (Did you know almost all of their vegetable side dishes have sugar in the ingredients?) Then, if you look at the copycat recipes online, most of them call for a can of condensed soup—no thank you, MSG and other unwanted additives! I knew there had to be a better way, and thankfully there is.

1. Preheat the oven to 350°F. Grease the baking dish with butter.

2. In a large sauté pan, melt the butter over medium heat. Add the onion and cook, stirring, until it softens but does not brown, 2 to 3 minutes. Throw in the garlic and cook for 1 minute, stirring.

3. Reduce the heat to medium-low and whisk in the flour. Stir constantly until the flour darkens but is not burned, 1 to 2 minutes. Whisk in the milk, salt, and pepper to taste and cook until it thickens slightly, about 1 minute.

4. Remove from the heat and, using a spatula or wooden spoon, stir in the Cheddar until it melts. Fold in the hash browns until evenly coated.

5. Transfer to the baking dish, taking care to push the thick mixture down to make an even layer.

6. Bake uncovered for 30 minutes, then turn on the broiler until the top turns golden brown, 3 to 4 minutes longer. Keep a close eye under the broiler so it doesn't burn! Serve warm with breakfast, lunch, or dinner.

Applesauce Oatmeal Pancakes

If you're looking for a nice twist on the usual pancakes, then I've got the recipe for you. These applesauce oatmeal pancakes incorporate rolled oats for added texture and applesauce for added sweetness (without any refined sugar!). This is definitely a recipe to double so you can freeze some for a rainy day. My daughters love these in their school lunches—I just cut them into strips and serve with yogurt for dipping.

1. In a large bowl, whisk together the flour, oats, baking powder, cinnamon, and salt. Make a well in the center and pour in the milk, applesauce, eggs, melted butter, and honey. Mix thoroughly with a fork until just combined, but do not overmix.

2. Heat a griddle to 350°F or a sauté pan over medium heat. Swirl enough butter around the griddle or pan to coat it well. Spoon out between ¼ and ⅓ cup of batter per pancake (depending on how big you like them!). When the pancakes have begun browning on the bottom and bubbling on the top, 2 to 3 minutes, flip and cook the other side for several more minutes. Transfer them to a plate and repeat to make the rest of the pancakes.

3. Serve with warm maple syrup and a side of fresh fruit.

Difficulty: Easy
Prep time: 10 minutes
Cook time: 10 to 15 minutes
Makes 4 or 5 servings

VEGETARIAN
NUT-FREE
FREEZER-FRIENDLY

1 cup whole wheat flour

½ cup rolled oats

2 teaspoons baking powder

1 teaspoon ground cinnamon

½ teaspoon salt

1 cup milk

½ cup homemade applesauce (page 147) or store-bought

2 eggs

3 tablespoons butter, melted, plus more for cooking

2 teaspoons honey

Warm maple syrup and fresh fruit, for serving

California Omelet

Difficulty: Easy
Prep time: 5 minutes
Cook time: 5 to 10 minutes
Makes 4 servings

GLUTEN-FREE
VEGETARIAN
NUT-FREE

8 eggs

1 tablespoon milk

Salt and ground black pepper

½ tablespoon butter

½ cup shredded Monterey Jack cheese

1 avocado, thinly sliced

Sour cream, for topping

This omelet is inspired by one I had for brunch at Uncle Bill's Pancake House in Manhattan Beach, California, when I was visiting my college buddy Christine years ago. Isn't it funny when a certain meal makes such a big impression? I hope you enjoy this combination as much as I did!

1. In a large bowl, whisk the eggs, milk, ⅛ teaspoon salt, and pepper to taste until well combined.

2. In a large sauté pan, melt the butter over medium heat. When the butter has melted but not yet browned, add the egg mixture. After about 30 seconds, tilt the pan while simultaneously using a spatula to push the edges of the omelet inward (toward the center of the pan). Tilting the pan will force the runny egg mixture to fill in around the edges. Repeat, while rotating the pan, until the egg is set and cooked all the way through, 2 to 3 more minutes.

3. Sprinkle the Monterey Jack over half the omelet and top that half with avocado slices. Fold the other half of the omelet over the top. Sprinkle with salt and pepper to taste and cut into 4 equal pieces. Serve immediately, topped with dollops of sour cream.

Sausage and Pepper Frittata

Frittatas are one of those wonderful dishes that can work for either breakfast or dinner (or lunch!). And with the addition of the sausage, peppers, mushrooms, and onion in this recipe, it can be an easy one-dish meal that'll satisfy your whole family.

1. Preheat the oven to 400°F.

2. In the medium ovenproof skillet, melt the butter over very low heat. Add the onion and let it cook slowly, stirring occasionally, until soft and translucent, 10 to 15 minutes. (To save time, I like to have the onion going in the pan while I chop and prepare the rest of the ingredients.)

3. Increase the heat to medium and add the sausage to the pan. Cook, stirring and breaking up the meat with a spatula, until mostly cooked through, 3 to 4 minutes. Add the bell pepper and mushrooms and cook, stirring occasionally, until the veggies are soft and the sausage is browned all the way through, another 5 minutes or so.

4. Spread the mixture evenly in the pan. Remove from the heat, pour the eggs over the filling, evenly sprinkle the Parmesan on top, and season with salt and pepper. Transfer to the oven and bake until the egg is firm, 20 to 25 minutes. Slice like a pie and serve warm.

"This one works great for breakfast or dinner (or lunch)!"

Difficulty: Easy
Prep time: 10 minutes
Cook time: 30 to 40 minutes (mostly hands off)
Seasonal note: Use locally grown peppers in the summer and fall months.
Makes 5 or 6 servings
Special tools needed: Ovenproof skillet

GLUTEN-FREE
NUT-FREE

1 tablespoon butter

½ onion, thinly sliced

2 links Italian sausage, casings removed

1 red bell pepper, cut into ¼-inch dice

4 ounces mushrooms, roughly chopped

8 eggs, lightly beaten

⅓ cup freshly grated Parmesan cheese

Salt and ground black pepper

Crunchy French Toast Casserole

Difficulty: Super easy
Prep time: 5 to 10 minutes
Cook time: 25 minutes
   (hands off)
Makes 4 or 5 servings
Special tools needed: 8- or
   9-inch square baking dish

GLUTEN-FREE (IF GLUTEN-FREE
   BREAD AND BREADCRUMBS
   ARE USED)
VEGETARIAN
NUT-FREE
FREEZER-FRIENDLY

1 tablespoon butter, melted,
plus more for greasing the
baking dish

5 or 6 slices whole wheat
bread, cut into 1-inch cubes
(about 5 cups)

3 eggs, beaten

½ cup milk

½ teaspoon pure vanilla extract

½ cup whole wheat
breadcrumbs

2½ teaspoons ground
cinnamon

French toast is already a pretty easy breakfast, but this baked casserole version is even easier than frying the bread in the pan. Be sure to double the recipe if you're feeding a crowd!

1. Preheat the oven to 350°F. Generously grease the baking dish with butter.

2. Spread the bread in the bottom of the prepared baking dish.

3. In a small bowl, whisk together the eggs, milk, and vanilla. Pour over the bread cubes and toss together.

4. In a small bowl, toss together the breadcrumbs and cinnamon, then stir in the melted butter to coat. Sprinkle in an even layer over the casserole.

5. Bake until golden brown and the egg mixture is cooked all the way through, about 25 minutes.

CHAPTER 3
lunch

lunch recipes

Veggie Cream Cheese

We found our new favorite snack food—and it's this cream cheese! It's fabulous as a dip for crackers or veggies, but (as you can see here) equally great on sandwiches with some thin cucumber slices for lunch. Also, if you're looking for some wholesome entertaining food for a wedding or baby shower, these would be super cute cut into little tea sandwiches and displayed on a pretty cake platter.

1. In the food processor, combine everything but the cream cheese and pulse until finely chopped.

2. Drop the cream cheese into the veggie mix and pulse until well combined. Serve or store in the fridge for up to 4 days.

Difficulty: Easy
Prep time: Less than 10 minutes
Cook time: N/A
Makes about 1½ cups
Special tools needed: Food
    processor

GLUTEN-FREE
VEGETARIAN
NUT-FREE

1 carrot, peeled and cut into large chunks

¼ cucumber, skin on, cut into large chunks

2 garlic cloves, smashed

1 green onion, white and green parts, roughly chopped

1 tablespoon chopped fresh dill

½ teaspoon salt

One 8-ounce package cream cheese, at room temperature

Sienna's Deviled Eggs

Both my kids like hard-boiled eggs—or the white part, at least. That is, unless the eggs are made into egg salad or deviled eggs. Then, magically, nothing goes to waste! Here's a real-food version of deviled eggs without store-bought mayo that's an all-time favorite of my daughter Sienna. She's now an absolute pro at making them! (Practice makes perfect, right?)

1. Lightly boil the eggs in water for 15 minutes. Run under cool water and peel.

2. Halve the eggs lengthwise and place the yolks in a small bowl. Mash the yolks with the back of a fork. Add the sour cream, oil, mustard, and salt and stir until well combined.

3. Spoon some yolk mixture into each white egg half. Sprinkle with paprika and serve, or refrigerate for up to 3 days.

Difficulty: Super easy
Prep time: 5 to 10 minutes
Cook time: 15 minutes
Makes 12 deviled eggs

GLUTEN-FREE
VEGETARIAN
NUT-FREE

6 eggs

1 tablespoon plus 1 teaspoon sour cream

1 tablespoon olive oil

½ teaspoon yellow mustard

⅛ teaspoon salt

Paprika, for garnish

LISA'S TIP: If you want "fancy" deviled eggs, then put the yolk mixture into a gallon ziplock bag, cut the corner off one end, and pipe the filling into the white egg halves.

Sour Cream and Onion Chicken Salad

I've tried making chicken salad all different ways (even using the dreaded processed store-bought mayo), and my older daughter has always claimed that she "doesn't like chicken salad." Well, that girl changed her mind super fast when one day I introduced this combination! This stuff is good with crackers, veggies, pretzels, and even just by itself. Trust me—give it a go and you'll see what all the fuss is about.

1. In a medium bowl, thoroughly mix together the chicken, sour cream, dried onion, onion powder, garlic powder, salt, and diced celery or carrots (if using).

2. Serve with crackers or veggie sticks or in a sandwich.

Difficulty: Super easy
Prep time: Less than 10 minutes
Cook time: N/A
Makes 3 or 4 servings

GLUTEN-FREE
NUT-FREE

2 cups shredded or diced cooked chicken (I highly recommend The Best Whole Chicken in the Slow Cooker, page 103)

½ cup sour cream

2 tablespoons dried minced onion or onion flakes

½ teaspoon onion powder

¼ teaspoon garlic powder

¼ teaspoon salt

Finely diced celery or carrots (optional)

Whole-grain crackers or fresh veggies, for serving

Broccoli Cheese Soup

If you're looking for creative ways to serve up vegetables, here's your answer! Please do me a favor, though, and don't lie to your reluctant eaters about the veggies in this dish. If you want to wait until after they gobble it up, that's fine, but make sure they know that the deliciousness in this soup is broccoli (and cheese and bacon, of course!).

1. In a large soup pot, cook the bacon over medium heat until browned and crisp, 3 to 4 minutes. Add the olive oil and onion and let it cook and soften for another minute.

2. Reduce the heat to medium-low, whisk in the flour, and cook, stirring or whisking constantly until the flour darkens in color, 1 to 2 minutes, taking care not to let the flour burn. Add the broccoli pieces, broth, milk, salt, and pepper to taste. Bring to a boil, then reduce to a simmer over medium-low and cook until the broccoli can be pierced easily with a fork, about 10 minutes.

3. Blend until smooth with the immersion blender (or in a stand blender in batches). Stir in the cream and Cheddar and serve warm. Garnish with extra bacon and cheese, if desired.

> "I love to pack my girls warm soup in Thermoses for school lunch!"

Difficulty: Medium
Prep time: Less than 10 minutes
Cook time: 20 minutes
Makes 6 to 8 servings
Special tools needed:
 Immersion blender or stand blender

NUT-FREE
FREEZER-FRIENDLY

3 slices bacon, cut into 1-inch pieces

1 tablespoon olive oil

¼ cup diced onion

3 tablespoons whole wheat flour

1 head broccoli (about 1¼ pounds), cut into 2-inch pieces

4 cups (32 ounces) chicken (page 103) or vegetable broth

1 cup milk (preferably whole)

½ teaspoon salt (or more to taste)

Ground black pepper

½ cup heavy cream

1 cup freshly shredded Cheddar cheese

Extra cooked bacon and shredded cheese, for garnish (optional)

Chicken Thai Pasta Salad

This hearty pasta salad can be thrown together in no time if you have some leftover cooked chicken on hand. And the flavor of the peanut butter helps to make it fairly kid-friendly (depending on the kid, of course!).

1. Put the cooked pasta in a large bowl and set aside.

2. In a small saucepan, combine the broth, peanut butter, and soy sauce and whisk over medium heat until well combined, 1 to 2 minutes.

3. Pour the peanut mixture over the noodles and mix thoroughly. Add the chicken, cucumber, green onions, and cilantro and toss to combine. Serve or store in the fridge for up to 4 days.

Difficulty: Easy
Prep time: 15 to 20 minutes
Cook time: N/A
Makes 4 or 5 servings

GLUTEN-FREE (IF GLUTEN-FREE
NOODLES AND SOY SAUCE
ARE USED)
DAIRY-FREE

3 cups (8 ounces) uncooked small pasta (such as penne or fusilli), cooked according to the package directions

¼ cup chicken broth, store-bought or homemade (page 103)

¼ cup peanut butter

¼ cup soy sauce (preferably reduced-sodium)

1½ cups cooked, shredded chicken (I recommend The Best Whole Chicken in the Slow Cooker, page 103)

½ cucumber, diced

¼ cup diced green onions, white and green parts

¼ cup chopped fresh cilantro

Taco Salad

Most kids love tacos, so this recipe is a great way to get kids to warm up to salad. It will quickly become a lunch box hit (yes, served cold)!

1. Preheat the broiler to high.

2. In a medium skillet, heat the oil over medium heat. Add the onion and cook, stirring, until it starts to soften, 2 to 3 minutes.

3. Add the beef and cook until browned and cooked through, 5 to 6 minutes, occasionally breaking it up with a spatula.

4. Meanwhile, place the tortillas on a large baking sheet and sprinkle them with a very light coating of Monterey Jack (reserving the rest for the salad). Sprinkle a few dashes of cumin on top of the cheese. Broil them until lightly browned, 2 to 3 minutes. Watch them carefully!

5. Add the beans to the beef and season the mixture with the cumin, chili powder, oregano, and salt and pepper to taste. Cook until heated through, then remove from the heat.

6. Spread the lettuce on a large serving platter, then top it with rows of tomatoes, the remaining Monterey Jack, and the sour cream. Add the cooked mixture in a row on the serving platter. Cut the tortillas into triangles (kitchen shears or a pizza cutter work great for this) and add them to the platter as well or, alternatively, add to separate lunch box compartments.

7. Sprinkle the entire dish with cilantro leaves, squeeze some lime juice over everything, and serve.

Difficulty: Easy
Prep time: 10 to 15 minutes
Cook time: 10 to 15 minutes
Makes 3 or 4 servings

GLUTEN-FREE
NUT-FREE

2 tablespoons olive oil

½ cup diced onion

½ pound ground beef

4 whole-grain corn tortillas

2 cups grated Monterey Jack cheese

½ teaspoon cumin, plus more for the tortillas

½ cup canned or cooked kidney, pinto, or black beans, drained and rinsed

¾ teaspoon chili powder

¼ teaspoon dried oregano

Salt and ground black pepper

1 head lettuce (any variety), washed and chopped

2 tomatoes, diced (or the pico de gallo from Fish Tacos, page 218)

½ cup sour cream

Leaves from 1 bunch cilantro

1 lime, halved

Black Bean "Hummus" Tartine

This open-faced sandwich was inspired by a lunch I had at Le Pain Quotidien in New York City. I love how it's not too hard to find a real-food lunch in the Big Apple!

1. To make the "hummus": In the food processor or blender, combine all the ingredients and puree. Add 1 or 2 tablespoons of water as needed to make it smooth.

2. To serve: Spread the hummus evenly on each slice of toast and top with sliced avocado and pimientos. Best right away but definitely within 24 hours. Hummus can alternatively be stored separate from bread for up to 4 days.

Difficulty: Easy
Prep time: 10 minutes
Cook time: N/A
Makes 4 or 5 servings
Special tools needed: Food processor or stand blender

GLUTEN-FREE (IF GLUTEN-FREE BREAD IS USED)
DAIRY-FREE
VEGETARIAN
NUT-FREE

"HUMMUS"

One 15-ounce can black beans, drained and rinsed

¼ cup chopped fresh cilantro leaves

¼ cup chopped green onions, white and green parts

2 tablespoons fresh lime juice

1 tablespoon olive oil

1 garlic clove, minced

½ jalapeño, seeded and minced

¼ teaspoon salt

FOR SERVING

4 or 5 pieces of whole wheat toast

1 avocado, sliced

One 4-ounce jar pimientos, drained

Caprese Pasta Salad

One of the reasons I love pasta salad is that it's an easy one-dish meal. A big thanks to my friend Carrie Vitt at Deliciously Organic for giving me the idea to turn one of my all-time favorites salads into this pasta salad! This is one of our go-to summer dishes when tomatoes are in season.

1. To make the pasta salad: In the large bowl, toss together all the ingredients.

2. To make the pesto: In the small food processor, puree the pesto ingredients.

3. Mix the pesto into the pasta salad until well combined. Garnish with fresh basil leaves.

LISA'S TIP: If peaches or nectarines are in season, they're a great addition to this recipe!

Difficulty: Easy
Prep time: Less than 20 minutes
Cook time: N/A
Makes 6 servings
Special tools needed: Small food processor

GLUTEN-FREE (IF GLUTEN-FREE PASTA IS USED)
VEGETARIAN

PASTA SALAD

8 ounces uncooked whole wheat pasta (such as penne, rigatoni, or macaroni), cooked according to the package directions

1½ cups diced tomatoes, any variety (about ¾ pound)

1 cup diced fresh mozzarella

2 handfuls fresh basil leaves, chopped

A few splashes balsamic vinegar, to taste

⅛ teaspoon salt

Ground black pepper, to taste

PESTO

1 cup (loosely packed) fresh basil leaves

3 tablespoons pine nuts

¼ cup freshly grated Parmesan cheese

1 garlic clove, roughly chopped

¼ cup olive oil

Couscous and Tomato Salad

One of the things I love about couscous is how little time it takes to cook—so you don't need to plan ahead! In less than 5 minutes you can have a tasty little side item that also keeps really well in the fridge if you want to have it on hand for the week.

1. Cook the couscous according to the package directions and set aside to cool.

2. Meanwhile, in a large bowl, combine the tomatoes, cucumber, feta, and olives (if using). Stir in the couscous.

3. In a small bowl, whisk together the oil, lemon juice, garlic, salt, dill, and pepper to taste. (You could also quickly shake up this dressing in a jar with a tight-fitting lid.) Pour on top of the couscous mixture and toss until well combined. Serve or refrigerate for up to 5 days.

Difficulty: Easy
Prep time: Less than 20 minutes
Cook time: 5 to 10 minutes
Makes 3 or 4 servings

VEGETARIAN
NUT-FREE

1 cup whole wheat couscous (I prefer pearl couscous, but the regular variety will also do)

½ pint cherry tomatoes, halved

½ cucumber, diced

½ cup crumbled feta cheese

½ cup pitted Greek olives, diced (optional, but recommended)

3 tablespoons olive oil

1 tablespoon fresh lemon juice

1 garlic clove, minced

½ teaspoon salt

¼ teaspoon dried dill

Ground black pepper

LISA'S TIP: The pictured lunch boxes are just serving suggestions. If you have a bigger appetite, feel free to supplement with an apple, a hard-boiled egg, or homemade trail mix!

Tangy Pasta Salad

I love pasta salads because they're easy to make and pretty filling. They also hold up really well in a packed lunch and give a nice break from a tired old sandwich. Even though this one is great for "adult" packed lunches, my kids scarf it down, too!

1. In a large bowl, toss together the pasta and spinach.

2. In a small bowl, whisk together the Parmesan, sour cream, lemon juice, olive oil, garlic, mustard, salt, and pepper to taste. Pour over the pasta mixture and toss until well combined. Serve or refrigerate for up to 5 days.

Difficulty: Easy
Prep time: 10 to 15 minutes
Cook time: N/A
Makes 3 or 4 servings

GLUTEN-FREE (IF GLUTEN-FREE
   PASTA IS USED)
VEGETARIAN
NUT-FREE

8 ounces whole-grain small pasta shapes (such as fusilli, mini penne, or elbow macaroni), cooked according to the package directions

2 cups spinach leaves, shredded (could substitute kale)

⅓ cup freshly grated Parmesan cheese

¼ cup sour cream

4 teaspoons fresh lemon juice

3 tablespoons olive oil

1 garlic clove, minced

2 teaspoons Dijon mustard

¼ teaspoon salt

Ground black pepper

Tarragon Chicken Salad

This chicken salad is inspired by a premade dish I used to buy at Publix, of all places. And since I pretty much gave up premade foods when I gave up processed foods, it was up to me to come up with a homemade alternative. But with this recipe, I don't feel like I'm missing a thing!

1. In a medium bowl, combine the chicken, almonds, sour cream, tarragon, mustard, salt, and pepper and mix well.

2. Serve with whole-grain crackers, bread, or lettuce (for wraps) or refrigerate for later.

Difficulty: Easy
Prep time: Less than 15 minutes
Cook time: N/A
Makes 4 or 5 servings

GLUTEN-FREE

2 cups cooked, shredded chicken (I highly recommend The Best Whole Chicken in the Slow Cooker; recipe follows)

¼ cup chopped or sliced almonds, lightly toasted in a dry skillet over medium-low heat or in a toaster oven, stirring frequently

¼ cup sour cream

1 teaspoon dried tarragon

½ teaspoon Dijon mustard

¼ teaspoon salt, or to taste

Ground black pepper, to taste

Whole-grain crackers, bread, or lettuce (for wraps), for serving

---

THE BEST WHOLE CHICKEN IN THE SLOW COOKER + HOMEMADE CHICKEN STOCK

This chicken is a staple in many of my recipes, so I'm repeating it from my first cookbook!

Peel 1 onion, cut it in half, and set it in a slow cooker. Combine 2 teaspoons paprika, 1 teaspoon salt, 1 teaspoon onion powder, 1 teaspoon dried thyme, ½ teaspoon garlic powder, ¼ teaspoon cayenne pepper, and ¼ teaspoon ground black pepper in a small bowl. Rub the spice mixture all over 1 whole chicken and place it on the onion. Cook on high for 4 hours or on low for 7 hours, or until the chicken is falling off the bone.

If you use chicken parts (such as 4 or 5 drumsticks) instead of a whole chicken, the cooking time will need to be slightly reduced.

To make homemade stock leave the bones, cooking juices, and everything else in the slow cooker after you pick out the good chicken. Fill it up with water and add the following: 1 (additional) halved onion, 1 roughly chopped carrot, 1 roughly chopped celery stalk, 1 thyme sprig, 1 parsley sprig, and 1 bay leaf. Turn on to low and cook overnight. In the morning, strain through a fine-mesh sieve and refrigerate or freeze the stock if you're not using it right away. Note: The sodium content will be significantly lower than store-bought broth, so you may need to add more salt than typically called for in a recipe.

Crab-Stuffed Avocados

If you're in a sandwich rut, this is a fun, light lunch to give you something different. The avocado shell holds everything together and the lime juice helps keep the avocado from browning until lunch time.

1. In a medium bowl, whisk together the yogurt, lime juice, and ginger. Stir in the crabmeat, bell pepper, cilantro, green onions, and sesame seeds. Season with salt and pepper to taste.

2. Halve the avocados, discard the pits, and evenly distribute the crab mixture on the cut sides. Refrigerate and eat within 24 hours.

> **LISA'S TIP:** I like to toast sesame seeds (or any raw seed or nut) in a dry skillet over medium-low heat or in a toaster oven while stirring frequently. Either way, it's important to keep a close eye on them because they can go from brown to burned very quickly!

"Treat yourself with this extra special lunch!"

Difficulty: Easy
Prep time: Less than 20 minutes
Cook time: N/A
Makes 4 servings

GLUTEN-FREE
NUT-FREE

1/4 cup plain yogurt

1 tablespoon plus 1 teaspoon fresh lime juice

1 1/2 teaspoons minced fresh ginger

Two 6-ounce cans crabmeat, drained and picked over

1/2 red bell pepper, diced

1/4 cup chopped fresh cilantro

2 tablespoons chopped green onions, white and green parts

1 teaspoon sesame seeds, lightly toasted

Salt and ground black pepper

2 large or 3 small avocados

CHAPTER 4
salads

salad recipes

Citrus Salad with Crispy Quinoa

Difficulty: Easy
Prep time: Less than 15 minutes
Cook time: 20 to 30 minutes
Makes 4 side servings
Special tools: Rimmed baking sheet

GLUTEN-FREE
DAIRY-FREE
VEGETARIAN
NUT-FREE

5 ounces spring lettuce mix (about 5 cups)

½ cup uncooked quinoa, cooked according to the package directions

2 oranges, peeled and diced

1 avocado, pitted, peeled, and diced

¼ cup chopped green onions, white and green parts

Citrus Vinaigrette (page 267)

This is a refreshing salad with a citrus-forward flavor. If you want to make it in advance, keep the dressing and quinoa separate until just before eating.

1. Put the lettuce in a large salad bowl and set aside.

2. Position a rack in the top third of the oven and preheat the broiler to high. Spread the cooked quinoa onto the rimmed baking sheet. Toast the quinoa under the broiler, stirring occasionally, until it begins to turn golden brown around the edges and to have a crispy texture, 10 to 12 minutes, checking frequently. Let cool, then add it to the lettuce mix.

3. Add the oranges, avocado, green onions, and dressing. Toss well to combine and serve immediately.

> **LISA'S TIP:** If your bulk bin quinoa doesn't come with directions, simply rinse and combine with 2 parts water (so the ½ cup above would be combined with 1 cup water) in a small pot with a tight-fitting lid. Bring to a boil, then reduce the heat to a simmer, cover and cook (just like rice) for 15 minutes.

Apple-Cheddar Side "Salad"

This may not be a typical salad, but it sure does a good job of highlighting how good apples and cheese are together! These happen to be two of my nine-year-old's favorite foods, so she gets very excited when I tell her this is going to be on the menu for dinner. This would be great leftover in the lunch box, too.

1. Core and cut the apples into ½-inch chunks. If using the corer/slicer tool, just cut the apple into the 8 (or 10) equal slices and then cut each slice into quarters.

2. In a large bowl, toss the apple chunks, Cheddar cubes, olive oil, lemon juice, and green onions. Serve immediately or refrigerate for up to 24 hours.

Difficulty: Super easy
Prep time: 10 to 15 minutes
Cook time: N/A
Makes 3 or 4 side servings
Special tools needed: Apple corer/slicer tool (helpful, not required)

GLUTEN-FREE
VEGETARIAN
NUT-FREE

1 pound (about 2 medium) apples (we like a mix in this recipe, such as Honeycrisp, Gala, Golden Delicious, or Granny Smith)

1 cup Cheddar cheese cubes (¼ inch)

1 tablespoon olive oil

1½ teaspoons fresh lemon juice

3 tablespoons chopped green onions, white and green parts

"This is an awesome salad that I love to devour!" —SIENNA LEAKE, AGE 9

Egg Salad with Bacon

Difficulty: Super easy
Prep time: 10 to 15 minutes
Cook time: N/A
Makes 4 or 5 servings

GLUTEN-FREE
NUT-FREE

8 eggs, hard-boiled (see Tip) and cooled

3 slices bacon, cooked and crumbled, 1 teaspoon bacon grease reserved

1 celery stalk, finely diced

¼ cup sour cream

2 teaspoons mustard (yellow or Dijon)

¼ teaspoon salt

Ground black pepper

Along with Sienna's Deviled Eggs (page 83), here's the other way my kids will eat the yolks in hard-boiled eggs. So these recipes are staples at our house!

1. Peel and dice the hard-boiled eggs. Try using a pastry blender for the dicing job!

2. In a medium bowl, gently mix the eggs with the bacon, bacon grease, celery, sour cream, mustard, salt, and pepper to taste. Serve or store covered in the refrigerator for up to 3 days.

> **LISA'S TIP:** To make hard-boiled eggs, cook them in lightly boiling water for 15 minutes, then run them under cool water. These are great to have on hand for snacks during the week!

Layered Jar Salad with White Beans

I would eat so many more vegetables if I had delicious jars of salad like this prepared in my fridge! It takes some planning, but trust me, it's worth it. Even my nine-year-old devoured this one. It was inspired by one of our favorite dips from my first cookbook.

1. To make the dressing: Whisk together all the ingredients. I like to emulsify mine by shaking it together for 1 or 2 minutes in a small jar. Divide the dressing among the four 1-quart jars.

2. To assemble the salad layers: On top of the dressing evenly distribute the rest of the layers in this order: onion, beans, tomato, arugula, and Parmesan.

3. Store in the fridge for up to 3 days and shake together just before serving. Eat straight out of the jar or transfer to a plate.

LISA'S TIP: Jar salads are a fun and easy way to prepare veggies for a busy day (or night!). Simply start by putting the dressing on the very bottom of the jar with one or two other "wet" ingredients for the next layer (such as beans, chickpeas, tomatoes, quinoa, or couscous). Throw in the greens next and then add grated cheese (if you wish) on top. Shake together just before serving.

"You can eat this one straight out of the jar or pour it out onto a plate first if you prefer."

Difficulty: Easy
Prep time: Less than 20 minutes
Cook time: N/A
Makes 4 servings
Special tools needed: Four 1-quart jars (wide mouth preferred) with lids

GLUTEN-FREE
DAIRY-FREE (IF THE PARMESAN IS OMITTED)
VEGETARIAN
NUT-FREE

DRESSING

¼ cup olive oil

2 tablespoons balsamic vinegar

2 tablespoons chopped fresh basil

1 garlic clove, minced

½ teaspoon salt

¼ teaspoon ground black pepper

SALAD LAYERS

½ cup diced red onion

One 15-ounce can cannellini beans, drained and rinsed

1 tomato, diced

8 cups (about one 5-ounce bag) fresh arugula

½ cup freshly grated Parmesan cheese

Asian Rice Noodle Salad

Difficulty: Easy
Prep time: 10 to 15 minutes
Cook time: Less than 5 minutes
  (depending on the rice
  noodle brand)
Makes 5 or 6 side servings

GLUTEN-FREE (IF GLUTEN-FREE SOY
  SAUCE IS USED)
DAIRY-FREE
VEGETARIAN

One 8-ounce box Asian brown
rice (whole-grain) noodles

¼ cup soy sauce (preferably
reduced-sodium)

1 tablespoon rice vinegar

2 teaspoons fresh lime juice
(from ½ lime)

2 teaspoons honey

2 teaspoons toasted sesame oil

1 teaspoon minced fresh ginger

1 garlic clove, minced

¾ cup fresh cilantro leaves,
chopped

¾ cup chopped salted, dry-
roasted peanuts or cashews

2½ cups coleslaw mix
(shredded green and red
cabbage plus carrots, found in
the produce aisle)

Red pepper flakes (optional)

The best thing about this salad is how it comes together in no time at all. Asian rice noodles generally cook more quickly than wheat noodles and with the addition of the precut coleslaw mix the prep time is very minimal. I recommend serving it with Coconut Shrimp (page 176)—what a yummy way to switch things up!

1. Cook the noodles according to the package directions. Drain and set aside in a large bowl to cool (a few minutes in the freezer can help!). Cut the noodles up a bit with kitchen shears or a knife to make them easier to toss.

2. In a small bowl, whisk together the soy sauce, vinegar, lime juice, honey, sesame oil, ginger, and garlic.

3. Add the sauce, cilantro, peanuts, and slaw mix to the bowl with the noodles and toss until well combined. If desired, sprinkle in red pepper flakes to taste. Serve at room temperature or refrigerate for later.

Feta and Avocado Pasta Salad

I would never have thought to put feta and avocado together before I tried them in a dip my friend Valerie made. I was sold—it's surprisingly good!

1. In a large bowl, toss together the pasta, avocados, feta, tomato, and parsley.

2. In a jar, combine the oil, lemon juice, garlic, and salt. Cover and shake vigorously until emulsified. Drizzle the dressing over the salad and mix until well combined.

Difficulty: Easy

Prep time: 15 to 20 minutes

Cook time: N/A

Seasonal note: Use locally grown tomatoes in the summer months.

Makes 4 or 5 servings

GLUTEN-FREE (IF GLUTEN-FREE PASTA IS USED)
VEGETARIAN
NUT-FREE

3 cups uncooked whole wheat pasta (such as penne or fusilli), cooked according to the package directions and cooled

2 avocados, pitted, peeled, and diced

1 cup crumbled feta cheese

1 cup diced tomato (from an 8-ounce tomato)

¼ cup fresh parsley leaves, chopped

¼ cup olive oil

2 tablespoons fresh lemon juice

2 garlic cloves, minced

¼ teaspoon salt

Roasted Summer Veggie Salad

VEGGIES

2 medium zucchini, trimmed and cut into 1-inch chunks

2 medium yellow summer squash, trimmed and cut into 1-inch chunks

1 pint grape or cherry tomatoes, halved

1 tablespoon olive oil

½ teaspoon salt

CROUTONS

3 slices whole wheat bread, cut into ½-inch cubes

3 garlic cloves, minced

2 tablespoons olive oil

¼ teaspoon salt

SALAD

1 cup freshly crumbled feta cheese

½ teaspoon grated lemon zest

¼ cup chopped fresh parsley leaves (optional)

Ground black pepper

This dish can either be served as a side salad or even as a main dish. I love how the fresh, bold flavors provide a nice change from the usual. This would be an excellent (and unexpected) addition to the spread at your next potluck event!

Difficulty: Medium
Prep time: 10 to 15 minutes
Cook time: Less than 30 minutes
Seasonal note: Use locally grown yellow squash, zucchini, and tomatoes in the summer months.
Makes 5 or 6 servings
Special tools needed: 9 x 13-inch baking dish, small rimmed baking sheet

GLUTEN-FREE (IF GLUTEN-FREE BREAD IS USED)
VEGETARIAN
NUT-FREE

1. For the veggies and croutons: Preheat the oven to 350°F.

2. In the baking dish, toss the veggies with the olive oil and salt.

3. On the small rimmed baking sheet, toss the bread cubes, garlic, olive oil, and salt until the bread is evenly coated.

4. Stick both the veggies and bread cubes in the oven side by side and cook until the croutons are golden brown, occasionally stirring to avoid burn spots on the edges, 16 to 18 minutes. Take out the croutons and set aside to cool.

5. Increase the oven temperature to 500°F and roast the veggies until they're easily pierced with a fork, 6 to 8 minutes.

6. Assemble the salad: In a large serving bowl, combine the veggies (minus any pan liquid), croutons, feta, lemon zest, parsley (if using), and pepper to taste. Serve warm, cold, or at room temperature.

Cobb Salad

This is one of the first salads I ever saw my kids enjoy (although they skipped the blue cheese!). I used to be guilty of thinking, "Oh, they're kids, they won't like salad," so I honestly never offered it to them. But when we cut out processed food, my mind-set changed, and eventually so did my kids' taste buds. They now love to chow down on all kinds of salads—a day I thought would never come!

Difficulty: Easy
Prep time: 15 to 20 minutes
Cook time: 5 minutes
Makes 4 or 5 servings

GLUTEN-FREE
NUT-FREE

1. Prepare the salad and toppings: In a skillet, cook the bacon over medium heat until crisp, 2 to 3 minutes per side. Drain the bacon on paper towels. When it is cool enough to handle, chop it into small pieces.

2. Arrange the lettuce on a large platter, then spread the bacon, eggs, avocados, tomatoes, pear, and blue cheese in rows over the lettuce.

3. Make the dressing: Whisk together the ingredients (or emulsify with an immersion blender) and serve on the side.

SALAD AND TOPPINGS

8 slices bacon

1 head lettuce (any variety), roughly chopped

3 eggs, hard-boiled (page 112), peeled, and diced

2 avocados, pitted, peeled, and diced

2 tomatoes (or equivalent amount of cherry tomatoes), diced

1 pear, cored and diced

3 to 4 ounces crumbled blue cheese

DRESSING

¼ cup olive oil

1 tablespoon red wine vinegar

1 teaspoon honey

½ teaspoon Dijon mustard

1 garlic clove, minced

¼ teaspoon salt

Ground black pepper, to taste

> **LISA'S TIP:** This would be great divided up into the lunch box, just like the Taco Salad on page 91.

Simple Salad Mix

Fresh salads with homemade dressings don't have to be complicated! I honestly first put together this combo because after a busy day I just didn't feel like making a full homemade dressing recipe. But my family loved this simple dish much more than I was expecting, so I knew I had to spread the word.

1. Remove the large stems from the kale. Chop the kale leaves and lettuce into bite-size pieces. I use my kitchen shears to "chop" my lettuce. You should have 8 or 9 cups salad greens.

2. In a small, dry skillet, toast the pine nuts over medium heat, stirring frequently and taking care that they don't burn, until they start to turn golden brown, 1 to 2 minutes. Season with salt and pepper to taste and remove from the pan so they don't continue to cook.

3. In the jar, combine the olive oil and lemon juice and shake vigorously until it emulsifies. Toss the dressing with the salad greens, Parmesan, and pine nuts until well combined and serve as soon as possible.

Difficulty: Super easy
Prep time: 5 to 10 minutes
Makes 4 or 5 servings
Special tools needed: Jar with a tight-fitting lid

GLUTEN-FREE
VEGETARIAN
NUT-FREE (IF PINE NUTS ARE OMITTED)

1 bunch lacinato (dinosaur) kale

1 head Bibb lettuce

⅓ cup pine nuts

Salt and ground black pepper

3 tablespoons olive oil

1 tablespoon fresh lemon juice

⅓ cup freshly grated Parmesan cheese

"Real food does not have to be complicated!"

CHAPTER 5

sides

side dish recipes

Lemon and Apple Coleslaw (Without Mayo)

I'm excited to present . . . coleslaw without mayo! Some people just don't like mayo, and others can't find an acceptable real-food version. This version solves both problems. I recommend pairing it with pulled pork or chicken and sweet Corn Muffins (page 169)—yum!

1. In a small bowl, whisk the sour cream, honey, mustard, vinegar, lemon juice, and salt until well combined.

2. In a large bowl, toss the coleslaw mix with the diced apple.

3. Pour the sour cream mixture on top, stir to combine, and serve or refrigerate for up to 2 days.

Difficulty: Super easy
Prep time: 10 to 15 minutes
Cook time: N/A
Seasonal note: Use locally grown cabbage in the winter months.
Makes 5 or 6 servings

GLUTEN-FREE
VEGETARIAN
NUT-FREE

½ cup sour cream

2 teaspoons honey

1 teaspoon Dijon mustard

1 teaspoon apple cider vinegar

1 tablespoon fresh lemon juice

½ teaspoon salt

6 cups coleslaw mix (shredded green and red cabbage plus carrots, found in the produce aisle)

1 apple, cored and diced (Fuji, Honeycrisp, or Gala recommended)

Lime and Cilantro Coleslaw

Difficulty: Super easy
Prep time: 10 to 15 minutes
Cook time: N/A
Seasonal note: Use locally grown cabbage in the winter months.
Makes 5 or 6 servings

GLUTEN-FREE
VEGETARIAN
NUT-FREE

6 cups coleslaw mix (shredded green and red cabbage plus carrots, found in the produce aisle)

½ cup chopped fresh cilantro

¼ cup diced green onions (white and green parts) or chives

½ cup sour cream

1 tablespoon fresh lime juice

2 teaspoons honey

½ teaspoon salt

The first time I served this Mexican-inspired coleslaw, my eleven-year-old said, "This is the only time I've ever liked coleslaw in my life." Oh, don't we mothers sometimes live for those moments! The flavors of this dish make it the perfect complement to any taco night, and it would make the perfect base for any taco salad as well.

1. In a large bowl, toss together the coleslaw mix, cilantro, and green onions.

2. In a small bowl, whisk the sour cream, lime juice, honey, and salt until well combined.

3. Thoroughly mix the dressing into the coleslaw mixture and serve or refrigerate for up to 2 days.

"The perfect complement to any taco night!"

"Rice" Pilaf

I don't have anything against brown rice other than the fact that it often takes a long time to cook (unless you can find the quick-cooking variety, which isn't always easy to do). So I use rice-shaped orzo pasta in this pilaf recipe, and my kids absolutely devour it!

1. In a dry medium skillet, lightly toast the almonds over medium heat, stirring often, until golden brown, 2 to 3 minutes. Remove from the pan and set aside.

2. In the same skillet, melt the butter, add the orzo, and cook, stirring, for a couple minutes to toast it. Pour in the broth, bring the mixture to a boil, then reduce the heat to low, cover, and cook until the pasta is tender, 14 to 16 minutes. Check on the orzo a couple of times and add a few more splashes of water or broth if necessary to keep it from sticking to the pan.

3. Stir in the almonds, season with salt and pepper to taste, and serve.

Difficulty: Easy
Prep time: 5 minutes
Cook time: 15 to 20 minutes
Makes 4 servings

GLUTEN-FREE (IF GLUTEN-FREE PASTA IS USED)
DAIRY-FREE (IF OLIVE OIL IS USED)
VEGETARIAN (IF VEGETABLE BROTH IS USED)

¼ cup sliced or slivered almonds

2 tablespoons butter or olive oil

1½ cups uncooked whole-grain orzo pasta

2 cups chicken (page 103) or vegetable broth

Salt and ground black pepper

Asparagus with Easy Dijon Sauce

Difficulty: Super easy

Prep time: 5 minutes

Cook time: 10 minutes

**Seasonal note: Use locally
grown asparagus when it's
available in the spring.**

Makes 4 or 5 servings

**Special tools needed: Steamer
basket**

GLUTEN-FREE
VEGETARIAN
NUT-FREE

1 pound asparagus, trimmed
or cut to fit a steamer basket

1 tablespoon butter

1 shallot, minced

⅓ cup heavy cream

½ teaspoon Dijon mustard

¼ teaspoon salt

I admit it, asparagus is not my favorite vegetable. But when it's topped with a sauce as delicious as this one, it really helps things. So if you already love asparagus, you'll be in heaven, and if you're really lucky, maybe your kids will eat a piece or two!

1. Pour 1 inch of water into a medium saucepan, set the steamer basket in the pan, and bring it to a boil over high heat. Reduce the heat to medium, add the asparagus, cover, and steam until tender when pierced with a fork, about 5 minutes. Remove from the pot immediately and keep warm.

2. In a small skillet, melt the butter over medium heat. Add the shallot and sauté, stirring often, until softened, 1 to 2 minutes. Add the cream, mustard, and salt and bring to a boil. Cook, stirring occasionally, until the liquid reduces by half, 2 to 3 minutes.

3. Pour the sauce over the cooked asparagus and serve.

Cauliflower Nuggets

Now, I'm not saying you can pass off cauliflower for chicken in this recipe, but the cooking method is similar to baked chicken nuggets and the outcome is surprisingly delicious. I grew up with my mom's breaded cauliflower and must confess it's a great way to get a good first impression of this vegetable. I'm not sure if I would've tried it as a kid without the breading, but now I'm a big fan of cauliflower no matter how it's cooked!

1. Preheat the oven to 450°F. Grease the large rimmed baking sheet with olive or avocado oil.

2. In a shallow bowl, beat the eggs. In another shallow bowl, combine the breadcrumbs, Parmesan, salt, and pepper. Set half the breadcrumb mixture aside in a separate bowl.

3. Designate one hand as your "wet hand" (for the eggs) and one as your "dry hand" (for the breadcrumbs). Using your wet hand, drop some cauliflower pieces into the egg mixture and coat them evenly. Shake off any excess egg, then drop the coated pieces into the breadcrumb mixture. Using your dry hand, sprinkle some breadcrumbs on top and roll them around until evenly coated. Transfer the coated pieces to the prepared baking sheet and repeat with the rest of the cauliflower (when you run out of breadcrumbs, use the second bowl—this keeps the crumbs from getting too soggy).

4. Brush or spray the top of the cauliflower pieces with a light coating of oil. Bake until the pieces can easily be pierced with a fork, about 20 minutes, flipping the pieces over halfway through. Serve warm.

Difficulty: Easy

Prep time: 10 to 15 minutes

Cook time: 20 minutes (hands off)

Seasonal note: Use locally grown cauliflower in the winter and spring months.

Makes 6 to 8 servings

Special tools needed: Large rimmed baking sheet

VEGETARIAN
NUT-FREE

Olive oil or avocado oil, for the pan and for brushing/spraying the cauliflower

3 eggs

1¼ cups finely ground whole wheat breadcrumbs

⅓ cup freshly grated Parmesan cheese

½ teaspoon salt, plus more to taste

Ground black pepper, to taste

1 head cauliflower, big stem removed, florets and smaller stems chopped into 1-inch pieces

Brussels Sprouts with Bacon and Apple Juice

Difficulty: Easy
Prep time: 10 minutes
Cook time: 10 to 15 minutes
Seasonal note: Use locally grown Brussels sprouts in the winter and spring months.
Makes 4 servings

GLUTEN-FREE
DAIRY-FREE
NUT-FREE

1 pound Brussels sprouts

2 slices bacon

⅓ cup apple juice

Salt and ground black pepper

I've tried Brussels sprouts so many different ways—roasted, boiled, and sautéed—and I've decided that simply cooking them on the stove with a couple lovely pieces of bacon and then finishing them off with some sweet apple juice hits the spot! Give it a go—I think you'll agree.

1. Trim the ends of the Brussels sprouts and pull off the outer leaves (if necessary), cut them in half, and set aside.

2. In a medium sauté pan, cook the bacon over medium heat until browned and cooked through, 2 to 3 minutes per side. Transfer the bacon to a plate lined with paper towels to cool, then crumble it.

3. Pour off all but 1 tablespoon of bacon grease from the pan. Set the skillet over medium heat, toss in the Brussels sprouts, and cook, stirring occasionally, until golden brown, 6 to 8 minutes.

4. Add the apple juice, cover, and steam until the liquid is almost completely absorbed and the sprouts are tender when pierced with a fork, 2 to 3 minutes. Check on the sprouts a couple times while they are steaming; if the liquid has already dried up, add a little water to the pan.

5. Transfer the sprouts to a serving bowl, top with the crumbled bacon, season with salt and pepper, and serve warm.

Simple Green Beans with Almonds

This is a simple side dish my mom used to make when I was a kid. How could I ever forget such an easy yet tasty combination? I'll eat twice as many green beans if they're prepared like this instead of plain!

1. Pour 1 or 2 inches of water into a medium saucepan, set the steamer basket in the pan, and bring it to a boil over high heat. Reduce the heat to medium, place the beans in the basket, cover, and steam until tender when pierced with a fork, 8 to 10 minutes.

2. In a small dry sauté pan, toast the almonds over medium-low heat, stirring often, until golden brown, 2 to 3 minutes.

3. In a serving bowl, toss the cooked green beans, toasted almonds, and soy sauce and serve warm.

"This is my favorite way to eat green beans!" —SYDNEY LEAKE, AGE 11

Difficulty: Super easy
Prep time: 5 minutes
Cook time: 10 to 15 minutes
Makes 5 or 6 servings
Special tools needed: Steamer basket

GLUTEN-FREE (IF GLUTEN-FREE SOY SAUCE IS USED)
DAIRY-FREE
VEGETARIAN

1 pound green beans, trimmed

¼ cup sliced almonds

2 teaspoons soy sauce (preferably reduced-sodium)

Italian-Spiced Zucchini

Difficulty: Super easy
Prep time: 5 to 10 minutes
Cook time: 5 to 10 minutes
**Seasonal note: Use locally
    grown zucchini in the
    summer months.**
Makes 4 or 5 servings

GLUTEN-FREE
DAIRY-FREE
VEGETARIAN
NUT-FREE

2 medium zucchini

1 tablespoon olive oil

½ teaspoon Italian seasoning

⅛ teaspoon salt

One of my favorite things about zucchini is that it takes no time at all to cook. Serve this with an easy main dish such as scrambled eggs, pasta, or pan-seared fish, and there's no excuse not to cook your own real food at home!

1. Trim the ends off the zucchini, halve them lengthwise, and cut crosswise into 1-inch chunks.

2. In a large sauté pan, heat the oil over high heat. Working in batches if necessary, sauté the zucchini until the underside begins to turn brown, about 2 minutes.

3. Using tongs or a spatula, flip each zucchini chunk over and sprinkle with the Italian seasoning and salt. Cook until the zucchini is browned on the bottom and can easily be pierced with a fork, about 2 minutes longer. Serve immediately.

The Easiest Homemade Applesauce—Ever!

If you're into kitchen projects that require minimal work, you'll love this one. This is seriously the easiest homemade applesauce ever . . . even easier than the stovetop version on my blog. You basically put the diced apples in the slow cooker and a few hours later—voilà! You have homemade applesauce. My kids especially love this one served warm.

1. Use the apple slicer/corer tool (if you have one) to cut the apples. I like to leave the peels on, but you can remove them if you prefer. If you don't have a slicer/corer, cut the apples into 8 (or 10) equal wedges. Cut each apple wedge in thirds to make 1-inch pieces.

2. Toss together the apples, lemon juice, and 1 tablespoon water in the slow cooker. Cover and cook on high for 3 hours, or until the apple chunks are so soft they break apart when you pierce them with a fork.

3. Mash the apples with a potato masher (or the back of a fork). If you left the peels on and really want to smooth things out, you can always use an immersion blender as well.

4. Serve warm with a little cinnamon (if using) sprinkled on top or store in the fridge or freezer for another day.

Difficulty: Super easy
Prep time: 10 to 15 minutes
Cook time: 3 hours on high
   (hands off)
Makes 3½ to 4 cups
Special tools needed:
   6- or 7-quart slow cooker;
   optional (but recommended):
   apple slicer/corer, potato
   masher

GLUTEN-FREE
DAIRY-FREE
VEGETARIAN
NUT-FREE
FREEZER-FRIENDLY

3 pounds apples, any variety or mix will do

1 teaspoon fresh lemon juice

Ground cinnamon, for serving (optional)

Simple Skillet Cornbread

Difficulty: Easy

Prep time: 5 to 10 minutes

Cook time: Less than
20 minutes

Makes 12 to 14 pieces

Special tools needed: 9-inch
cast-iron skillet (make sure
it's seasoned)

GLUTEN-FREE
VEGETARIAN
NUT-FREE
FREEZER-FRIENDLY

2 cups finely ground cornmeal

1 teaspoon salt

½ teaspoon baking powder

½ teaspoon baking soda

1½ cups buttermilk

2 eggs, beaten

5 tablespoons butter, melted

This skillet cornbread is super easy to make and would be a great complement to dishes like Easy Slow Cooker Steak Chili (page 197), Lentil and Sausage Stew (page 186), Slow Cooker Black Bean Soup (page 192), and, of course, pulled pork or barbecue!

1. Preheat the well-seasoned cast-iron skillet in a 450°F oven for at least 10 minutes while you prepare the batter.

2. In a large bowl, whisk together the cornmeal, salt, baking powder, and baking soda. Make a well in the center of the mixture and drop in the buttermilk, eggs, and melted butter. Use a fork to mix the wet and dry ingredients together until thoroughly combined.

3. Pour the cornbread batter into the hot skillet (I sometimes don't even take it out of the oven to do this) and bake until the cornbread is golden brown and a toothpick inserted in the center comes out clean, 15 to 18 minutes.

4. Serve warm and freeze the leftovers for a rainy day!

Sydney's Roasted Potatoes

My eleven-year-old daughter, Sydney, absolutely loves roasted potatoes. Whether fingerling, new, or another variety of small potatoes, she doesn't discriminate. This dish is a great reminder that real food doesn't have to be complicated!

1. Preheat the oven to 425°F.

2. Slice the potatoes in half (lengthwise if using fingerling potatoes).

3. On the rimmed baking sheet, toss the potatoes with the olive oil, herbs, garlic salt, and pepper. Bake until tender when pierced with a fork, 20 to 25 minutes, tossing them once or twice.

Difficulty: Super easy
Prep time: Less than 10 minutes
Cook time: 20 to 25 minutes
Makes 4 or 5 servings
Special tools needed: Rimmed baking sheet

GLUTEN-FREE
DAIRY-FREE
VEGETARIAN
NUT-FREE

1½ pounds small potatoes (such as fingerling, new, or other small potatoes)

1 tablespoon olive oil

1 teaspoon chopped fresh rosemary leaves

½ teaspoon chopped fresh thyme leaves

½ teaspoon garlic salt

½ teaspoon ground black pepper

CHAPTER 6

snacks and appetizers

snack and appetizer recipes

Toasted Coconut Chips

My daughters would happily eat unsweetened coconut flakes plain, but then I discovered how delicious they taste toasted with a little extra flavor! While these are great by the handful, the fun part of this recipe is really all the things you can do when they're done. They're fabulous mixed into a homemade trail mix or used as a topping on a variety of things, including Our Favorite Overnight Oats (page 62), ice cream, yogurt, and more.

Difficulty: Super easy
Prep time: 5 minutes
Cook time: 5 to 10 minutes
Makes about 1 cup
Special tools needed: Small rimmed baking sheet and parchment paper

GLUTEN-FREE
DAIRY-FREE
VEGETARIAN

1 cup unsweetened large coconut flakes

½ teaspoon ground cinnamon

Pinch of salt

1 to 2 teaspoons honey (just enough to lightly coat)

1. Preheat the oven to 350°F.

2. In a medium bowl, toss the coconut flakes with the cinnamon and salt. Drizzle in the honey and mix thoroughly.

3. Spread the coconut in an even layer on the small rimmed baking sheet lined with parchment paper. Bake for 3 to 4 minutes, stir, and check the progress. Bake until golden brown, 1 to 2 minutes longer. The coconut can quickly go from golden to burned, so check on it frequently during the last couple minutes! Let cool, then store in an airtight container at room temperature for up to 1 week.

"I always pick the coconut out of Mom's granola (to eat), so when she made this recipe I was in heaven!"

—SYDNEY LEAKE, AGE 11

No-Bake Peanut Butter Oat Bars

Difficulty: Super easy

Prep time: 10 to 15 minutes

"Cook" time: Refrigerate for at least 1 hour

Makes 16 to 20 bars

Special tools needed: 8- or 9-inch square baking dish and wax paper or parchment paper

GLUTEN-FREE (IF GLUTEN-FREE OATS AND CEREAL ARE USED)
DAIRY-FREE
VEGETARIAN

1½ cups peanut butter (could sub sunflower seed or almond butter for those with allergies)

6 tablespoons pure maple syrup

1 cup rolled oats

1 cup crunchy flax cereal (or other small whole-grain cereal—I used Enjoy Life brand) or nuts

I love it when I have a batch of these bars on hand because then I'm prepared with yummy, filling snacks when I hear the inevitable "I'm hungry. . . ." These bars are also great to supplement a lunch or to eat as a quick breakfast with a side of fruit. I think the moral of the story is that it's hard to go wrong with this recipe, so I hope you and your family enjoy them just as much as we do!

1. Line the bottom and sides of the baking dish with wax paper or parchment paper.

2. In a large bowl, mix the peanut butter and maple syrup thoroughly with a rubber spatula. Pour in the oats and cereal and mix until well combined.

3. Spread the bar mixture in the pan in an even layer. Refrigerate for at least 1 hour. Cut and serve or store in the fridge.

"These will quickly solve those 'I'm hungry . . .' complaints!"

Honeydew Green Smoothie

Smoothies are always a big help when it comes to "eating your greens," and this recipe is no exception. The vibrant green spinach paired with the pale-colored melon really makes for a pretty outcome. If you have reluctant little ones who might turn their noses up at something green, you can try giving it a fun nickname (such as the Incredible Hulk Potion!) or putting it in a special, new opaque cup. Just make sure to show them what they were drinking afterward so they know what tasted so good!

In a blender, combine 1 cup water, the bananas, spinach, honeydew, pineapple, and ice cubes, and blend until smooth. Serve immediately or store in fridge for up to 24 hours.

Difficulty: Super easy

Prep time: 5 to 10 minutes

Cook time: N/A

Makes 3 or 4 servings

Special tools needed: Blender

GLUTEN-FREE
DAIRY-FREE
VEGETARIAN
NUT-FREE
FREEZER-FRIENDLY

2 bananas (the riper, the sweeter!)

1½ cups spinach leaves

1 cup diced honeydew melon

1 cup diced frozen or fresh pineapple

½ cup ice cubes

Whole Wheat Lemon Raspberry Muffins

Difficulty: Medium
Prep time: 10 minutes
Cook time: 18 to 20 minutes
Makes 12 muffins
Special tools needed: Electric mixer, Microplane or zester, muffin tin, paper or silicone muffin liners

VEGETARIAN
NUT-FREE
FREEZER-FRIENDLY

1½ cups whole wheat flour

1 teaspoon baking soda

½ teaspoon salt

1½ teaspoons grated lemon zest

1 stick (4 ounces) butter, at room temperature (but not melted)

1 egg

½ cup pure maple syrup

½ cup milk

1 teaspoon pure vanilla extract

1 cup frozen raspberries (no need to thaw)

This is one of our favorite muffin recipes! The raspberries and lemon complement each other very well, but if you prefer blueberries instead—I promise, it won't disappoint.

1. Preheat the oven to 350°F. Line 12 cups of the muffin tin with paper or silicone liners.

2. In a medium bowl, whisk together the flour, baking soda, salt, and lemon zest.

3. With the electric mixer fitted with the whisk (or beaters), cream the butter on medium speed until smooth. Reduce the speed to low and slowly add in the egg, maple syrup, milk, and vanilla, scraping the sides of the bowl as necessary. With the speed still on low, slowly add in the flour. The batter will be slightly thick. Carefully fold in the raspberries with a spatula until well combined.

4. Divide the batter evenly among the muffin cups (a small ice cream scoop makes this easy). Bake until a toothpick inserted in the center comes out clean, 18 to 22 minutes.

> **LISA'S TIP:** I've found that a rasp-style zester, such as a Micro-plane, is the best tool for grating citrus zest.

Apple and Banana Kabobs with Peanut Butter Dip

This is a snack my kids will gobble up in no time. It's funny how my older daughter will sometimes tell me she doesn't like apples, but if a tasty dip is involved? She forgets all about that claim (ha ha).

1. In a small bowl, combine the peanut butter, coconut milk, honey, and vanilla and whisk with a fork until thoroughly combined. Add a few more splashes of coconut milk to help loosen the mixture and make it easier to stir if necessary.

2. Cut the apple and bananas into ½- or 1-inch pieces. Alternate them on wooden skewers and serve with the dip on the side.

LISA'S TIP: Peanut butter is one of those store-bought foods that should (ideally) contain only one ingredient: peanuts! Check the back of the jar to see how it measures up. You'd be surprised how many brands include unnecessary extras.

Difficulty: Super easy
Prep time: Less than 10 minutes
Cook time: N/A
Makes 2 or 3 servings
Special tools needed: Small wooden skewers

GLUTEN-FREE
DAIRY-FREE
VEGETARIAN

½ cup peanut butter

¼ cup coconut milk (a little more if your peanut butter is extra thick and chunky)

1 teaspoon honey

¼ teaspoon pure vanilla extract

1 large apple

2 bananas

Copycat Cashew Cookie "LÄRABAR"

Difficulty: Easy
Prep time: 10 to 15 minutes
Cook time: N/A
Makes 12 bars
Special tools needed: Food processor

GLUTEN-FREE
DAIRY-FREE
VEGETARIAN
FREEZER-FRIENDLY

1 cup dried Medjool dates, pitted

1 cup raw cashews

¼ cup peanut butter

Store-bought LÄRABARs are such a simple snack, using only a few whole ingredients, which means they're easy to make at home as well. And, as with most things, it's hard to beat the taste of homemade! My daughters seriously love these things.

1. In the food processor, combine the dates, cashews, peanut butter, and 1 tablespoon water and puree until the mixture starts to stick together. Add a little more water if necessary to help the mixture come together.

2. Use your hands to squeeze the date mixture into one big clump. Mash it down on a cutting board or sheet of wax paper to form an even rectangle about ½ inch thick, using the sides of your hands (or a knife) to make the edges straight. Cut it into 12 even squares. (As an alternative, you could roll the mixture into balls.) For best results, store in the fridge, although the bars can be kept at room temperature.

Corn Muffins

These muffins are a little on the sweeter side compared to typical cornbread, which make them great little snacks by themselves or fabulous as a complement to a variety of hearty soups (check out the Soups and Stews chapter on page 181)! No matter what you do with them, I think you'll be pleased with how quick and easy they are to make.

1. Preheat the oven to 400°F. Line 12 cups of the muffin tin with silicone or paper liners.

2. In a large bowl, whisk together the cornmeal, flour, baking powder, and salt. Make a well in the center and pour in the melted butter, honey, eggs, and milk. Stir with a fork until just combined. Fold in the corn kernels.

3. Divide the batter evenly among the muffin cups (a small ice cream scoop makes this job easy!) and bake until golden brown, 15 to 18 minutes. Serve warm and be sure to reheat the leftovers before serving.

Difficulty: Easy
Prep time: 10 minutes
Cook time: 15 minutes
Makes 12 muffins
Special tools needed:
  Muffin tin, silicone or paper
  muffin liners

VEGETARIAN
NUT-FREE
FREEZER-FRIENDLY

¾ cup finely ground cornmeal

¾ cup whole wheat flour

2 teaspoons baking powder

½ teaspoon salt

1 stick (4 ounces) butter, melted

¼ cup honey

2 eggs, beaten

½ cup milk

¾ cup frozen corn kernels
(no need to thaw)

Smoked Salmon Dip

Difficulty: Super easy

Prep time: Less than 15 minutes

Cook time: N/A

Makes about 1¾ cups

Special tools needed: Food processor

GLUTEN-FREE (IF GLUTEN-FREE CRACKERS ARE USED)

NUT-FREE

4 ounces smoked salmon (if using canned, drain it first)

One 8-ounce package cream cheese

2 tablespoons butter, melted

¼ cup diced red onion

2 tablespoons capers, drained, plus more for garnish

Celery sticks and whole-grain crackers, for serving

This is a fabulous dip, whether for a party or potluck or just to have in your fridge when you're hungry for a snack. I've even substituted smoked trout (minus the capers) and it was just as tasty!

In the food processor, combine the salmon, cream cheese, melted butter, onion, and capers and process until smooth. Garnish with capers and serve with celery and crackers. Can be stored in the fridge for up to 3 days.

Easy Baked Falafel (Chickpea Cakes)

Oil, for greasing the baking sheet (I like avocado spray)

DIPPING SAUCE (COULD ALTERNATIVELY USE TZATZIKI SAUCE, PAGE 275)

¼ cup plain yogurt

2 tablespoons tahini

1 tablespoon fresh lemon juice

CHICKPEA CAKES

Two 15-ounce cans chickpeas, drained and rinsed

3 tablespoons whole wheat flour

2 tablespoons chopped fresh dill, plus extra (optional) for serving

4 cloves garlic, minced

2 green onions, white and green parts, roughly chopped

2 teaspoons ground cumin

¾ teaspoon salt

½ teaspoon ground black pepper

I realize I may be late to the party here, but falafel is awesome stuff. It was served to us after a five-day hike (called the "W Trek") in Patagonia, which was the trip of a lifetime, by the way, and those things were gone like hot cakes. Literally. So I came home determined to make some myself and had no idea how easy they were (or how well they would hold up in the fridge). You'll be glad to have some of these on hand next time hunger strikes.

Difficulty: Easy
Prep time: 5 to 10 minutes
Cook time: 25 minutes
Makes 16 to 18 three-inch patties
Special tools needed: Large baking sheet and food processor

GLUTEN-FREE (IF GLUTEN-FREE FLOUR REPLACEMENT IS USED)
DAIRY-FREE (IF DIPPING SAUCE IS OMITTED)
VEGETARIAN
NUT-FREE
FREEZER-FRIENDLY

1. Preheat the oven to 425°F. Grease the large baking sheet.

2. Make the dipping sauce: In a small bowl, whisk together the yogurt, tahini, and lemon juice. Set aside.

3. Make the chickpea cakes: In the bowl of the food processor, use a spoon to toss together the chickpeas, flour, dill, garlic, green onions, cumin, salt, and pepper. Pulse until well combined.

4. Shape the mixture into 16 to 18 three-inch patties by squeezing each one together in your hands and then flattening them out onto the prepared baking sheet. Grease the tops with a little oil (I love my avocado oil spray for this purpose) and bake until golden brown on the bottom, 12 to 14 minutes. Flip over the patties and bake until golden brown on the second sides, 12 to 14 minutes longer.

5. Serve warm or at room temperature with the dipping sauce and garnish with extra dill, if desired.

Zucchini Stacks

This recipe was inspired by the Shortcut Eggplant Parmesan in my first cookbook because cooking veggies like this is Oh. So. Good! We sometimes have these as a little appetizer (and by appetizer I mean they're all gone by the time we sit down at the table with the rest of our food!), but they'd also be great as a side dish or even as a topping over cooked pasta or a salad. No matter what you do with them, they won't last long.

1. Trim the zucchini, halve them crosswise, and cut them into thirds lengthwise to give you 12 long strips (6 per zucchini). Thinly slice the mozzarella into 12 long strips and set aside.

2. Spread the flour onto a plate and dredge the zucchini in the flour to coat both sides.

3. In a large sauté pan (with a tight-fitting lid), heat a thin layer of olive oil over medium heat. Add the zucchini strips, working in batches so as not to overcrowd them. (It's helpful to rinse and wipe out the pan and add fresh olive oil with each batch.) Cook until the bottoms are golden brown, 2 to 3 minutes. Flip the zucchini over and, working very quickly, top each piece with a dollop of marinara sauce and a strip of mozzarella. Cover the pan and cook until the cheese is melted, the bottom of the zucchini is browned, and the zucchini can be pierced with a fork, 30 seconds to 1 minute.

4. Transfer to a plate lined with paper towels, sprinkle with salt to taste, and cover with foil to keep warm. Repeat to make the remaining zucchini stacks.

Difficulty: Easy
Prep time: 5 to 10 minutes
Cook time: 5 to 10 minutes
Makes 3 or 4 servings

VEGETARIAN
NUT-FREE

2 zucchini (about 1 pound total)

6 ounces mozzarella cheese

¼ cup whole wheat flour

Olive oil, for cooking

½ cup marinara sauce (page 280)

Salt

Coconut Shrimp

Difficulty: Easy
Prep time: 10 minutes
Cook time: 5 to 10 minutes
Makes 4 or 5 servings

DAIRY-FREE

¾ cup unsweetened shredded coconut

⅓ cup whole wheat flour

1 egg

1 pound shrimp, peeled, deveined, and patted dry

3 tablespoons coconut oil or butter

Salt

Funnily enough, I'm not a fan of raw coconut (I despise coconut cakes), but oh how I love toasted coconut. The taste is just transformed when it's cooked, and it's also the perfect complement to what would otherwise have been plain old shrimp. So make this for a fun appetizer, or spice up your next weeknight dinner by serving it with Asian Rice Noodle Salad (page 116) and some simple steamed green beans. It will not disappoint!

1. In a medium bowl, combine the coconut and flour and mix well. In another medium bowl, beat the egg.

2. Designate one hand as your "wet hand" (for the egg) and one as your "dry hand" (for the coconut mixture). Using your wet hand, pick up a shrimp, drop it into the egg bowl, and stir around to coat. Let any excess egg drip off, then drop it into the coconut mixture. Using your dry hand, push the coconut mixture onto both sides of the shrimp until well coated. Transfer the shrimp to a clean plate and repeat with the rest of the shrimp.

3. In a large sauté pan, heat the coconut oil over medium-high heat. Add the shrimp in one layer (or hold some back to cook in a second batch, adding more oil if necessary). Cook until golden brown and cooked all the way through, 2 to 3 minutes per side. Salt the shrimp to taste and serve warm or at room temperature.

Moroccan Meatballs

Difficulty: Easy
Prep time: 15 to 20 minutes
Cook time: 10 to 12 minutes
Makes 4 entrée servings or
    6 appetizer servings
Special tools needed: Rimmed
    baking sheet and toothpicks

DAIRY-FREE (OMIT THE DIPPING
    SAUCE)
NUT-FREE
FREEZER-FRIENDLY

Olive oil, for the baking sheet

1 pound ground beef (ground
lamb is also great in this
recipe!)

½ cup minced onion

½ cup fresh mint leaves,
chopped

½ cup fresh parsley leaves,
chopped

1 egg

3 garlic cloves, minced

3 tablespoons whole wheat
breadcrumbs

1½ teaspoons ground cumin

1 teaspoon ground cinnamon

½ teaspoon salt

Ground black pepper

Tzatziki Sauce (optional;
page 275), for serving

This recipe with bold Moroccan flavors is a fun way to switch things up. Even though I'm including it as an appetizer, it could easily become a main dish along with some sides (I recommend whole wheat couscous and veggies). My kids especially love this recipe and fight over who gets the last meatball!

1. Preheat the oven to 425°F. Grease the rimmed baking sheet with olive oil.

2. In a large bowl, use your hands to combine all the ingredients except the tzatziki. Roll the mixture into meatballs the size of golf balls and place them in rows on the prepared baking sheet. (This is a fun job for little ones.)

3. Bake until the meatballs are brown all the way through, 10 to 12 minutes. Pierce with toothpicks and serve warm with the tzatziki sauce, if desired.

LISA'S TIP: I love to "chop" my fresh herbs with kitchen shears—works great!

"These also work great as a main dish!"

CHAPTER 7

soups and stews

soup and stew recipes

Quick Cauliflower Soup

This is a quick and easy soup for a busy winter weeknight. But if you're feeling adventurous and have a little more time, double or triple the recipe so you can save some in the freezer for a rainy day!

1. In a medium soup pot, heat the olive oil over medium heat. Add the onion and cook until it softens but does not brown, a few minutes.

2. Add the cauliflower, lemon pepper, salt, and nutmeg and cook, stirring occasionally, until the cauliflower begins to brown, 4 to 5 minutes.

3. Add the broth and bring to a boil, then reduce the heat to a simmer, cover, and cook until the cauliflower is soft when pierced with a fork, 10 to 15 minutes.

4. While the soup is cooking, lightly toast the chopped walnuts in a small dry pan over low heat until they slightly darken in color, 3 to 4 minutes.

5. Blend soup until smooth with the immersion blender (or in the stand blender in batches). Ladle into bowls, top with the toasted walnuts, and serve warm.

Difficulty: Easy

Prep time: 10 minutes

Cook time: Less than 20 minutes

Seasonal note: Use locally grown cauliflower in the winter months.

Makes 4 or 5 servings

Special tools needed: Immersion or stand blender

GLUTEN-FREE
DAIRY-FREE
VEGETARIAN (IF VEGETABLE BROTH IS USED)
NUT-FREE (IF WALNUTS ARE OMITTED)
FREEZER-FRIENDLY

1½ tablespoons olive oil

½ cup diced onion

1 head cauliflower, chopped into florets

¾ teaspoon lemon pepper seasoning

¾ teaspoon salt (or more to taste)

⅛ teaspoon ground nutmeg

3 cups chicken (page 103) or vegetable broth

½ cup chopped walnuts

Lentil and Sausage Stew

Difficulty: Easy
Prep time: 5 minutes
Cook time: 30 to 35 minutes
  (mostly hands off)
Seasonal note: Use locally
  grown carrots in the winter
  months.
Makes 6 or 7 servings (enough
  for leftovers!)

GLUTEN-FREE
DAIRY-FREE
NUT-FREE
FREEZER-FRIENDLY

1 tablespoon olive oil

½ onion, diced

4 carrots, peeled and diced

3 garlic cloves, minced

1 pound bulk Italian sausage
(I prefer mild), or links with
casings removed

1½ cups dried green lentils,
rinsed

1 bay leaf

½ teaspoon dried thyme

¼ teaspoon ground black
pepper

6 cups chicken (page 103)
or vegetable broth

Salt

Carrot ribbons (made with
vegetable peeler), for garnish
(optional)

Growing up, my husband loved when his mom made lentils, sausage, and biscuits for dinner. When we were newlyweds, this was a meal I wasted no time trying to re-create. I went out and bought a can of lentil soup, a package of precooked factory-farmed sausage, and a tube of processed biscuits—don't judge, I honestly didn't know any better at the time! So, many years later (and wiser—thank goodness), here is a revised deeeelicious version of his childhood favorite. If you still want the biscuits on the side, make them from scratch with whole wheat flour—go for it!

1. In a large pot, heat the oil over medium heat. Stir in the onion, carrots, and garlic and cook, stirring occasionally, until the onion is softened, 2 to 3 minutes.

2. Add the sausage and cook, stirring and breaking it up occasionally, until it is cooked all the way through, 5 to 6 minutes. If desired, drain off and discard the fat.

3. Pour in the lentils, seasonings, and broth and bring to a boil. Reduce to a simmer and cook until the lentils are tender, 20 to 25 minutes. Add salt to taste and serve warm or freeze for another day. (It can be stored in the fridge as well, of course.) Garnish with carrot ribbons, if desired.

> **LISA'S TIP:** Try the easiest biscuits ever with this dish, which can be found by typing "cream biscuits" into the search bar on my blog, 100daysofrealfood.com.

White Chicken Chili

Difficulty: Easy
Prep time: 10 to 15 minutes
Cook time: Less than
     30 minutes
Makes 4 servings

GLUTEN-FREE
NUT-FREE
FREEZER-FRIENDLY

1 tablespoon olive oil

½ onion, diced

½ jalapeño, minced

1 pound boneless, skinless
chicken breasts, cut into 1-inch
pieces

1 garlic clove, minced

1 teaspoon chili powder

1 teaspoon ground cumin

1¼ teaspoons salt

¼ teaspoon cayenne pepper

½ cup frozen corn kernels
(no need to thaw)

Two 15-ounce cans white beans
(such as Great Northern or
cannellini), drained and rinsed

1¾ cups chicken broth,
store bought or homemade
(page 103)

¼ cup heavy cream

TOPPINGS: Chopped cilantro,
sour cream, grated Monterey
Jack cheese, diced avocado,
and/or corn tortilla strips

Whether you call this dish a chili or hearty chicken and bean stew, it's definitely a winner. The first time I made it for my kids, they asked me so many times what it was called, but by the end of the meal they cared much more about getting second helpings than remembering the name! If you have time be sure to double the recipe and store in the fridge or freezer, because, like most soups and stews, the leftovers are amazing.

1. In a medium soup pot, heat the olive oil over medium heat. Add the onion and jalapeño and cook, stirring, until the onion has softened, 2 to 3 minutes.

2. Add the chicken and cook, stirring occasionally, until it is lightly browned on the outside and no longer pink on the inside (add more olive oil if the pot starts to dry out), 4 to 5 minutes.

3. Toss the minced garlic and spices into the pot and turn a few times to coat the chicken evenly. Add the corn, beans, and chicken broth and bring to a boil. Reduce the heat to low and simmer, about 20 minutes.

4. Break up some of the beans with the back of a wooden spoon to help thicken the chili. Stir in the cream, garnish with the desired toppings, and serve!

LISA'S TIP: This dish is also great with leftover cooked chicken. Just skip step 2 and add the cooked chicken with the garlic and spices in step 3.

Kale, Sausage, and White Bean Soup

This is a one-dish meal that can be ready in no time at all! It's a great way to warm up on a cold winter day. And it's also a great way to get in your quota of leafy greens for the day!

1. In a large soup pot, heat the oil over medium heat. Add the onion and garlic and cook, stirring occasionally, until the onion is softened, 2 to 3 minutes. Add the sausage and cook until it is cooked all the way through (no longer pink), 5 to 10 minutes.

2. Meanwhile, strip and discard the thick ribs from the kale and cut the leaves into shreds (I like to use kitchen shears for this job).

3. Add the broth, kale, beans, salt, and pepper to taste to the pot and bring to a boil. Reduce the heat to a simmer and cook until the kale is wilted, 5 to 10 minutes. Serve warm and enjoy!

Difficulty: Easy
Prep time: 5 to 10 minutes
Cook time: 20 to 25 minutes
Makes 4 servings

GLUTEN-FREE
DAIRY-FREE
NUT-FREE
FREEZER-FRIENDLY

1 tablespoon olive oil

½ onion, diced

2 garlic cloves, minced

1 pound mild or hot Italian sausage links, cut into ¾- to 1-inch chunks

1 bunch kale

6 cups chicken broth, store bought or homemade (page 103)

Two 15-ounce cans white beans (such as cannellini), drained and rinsed

1 teaspoon salt

Ground black pepper

Slow Cooker Black Bean Soup

Difficulty: Super easy

Prep time: Less than 15 minutes

Cook time: 8 to 10 hours on high (hands off)

Makes 4 or 5 servings

Special tools needed: 6- or 7-quart slow cooker, immersion or stand blender

GLUTEN-FREE
DAIRY-FREE (OMIT THE SOUR CREAM AND CHEESE TOPPINGS)
VEGETARIAN
NUT-FREE
FREEZER-FRIENDLY

1½ cups dried black beans (rinsed and picked over to remove any discolored or grossly misshapen beans— or sometimes even pebbles!)

4 cups chicken (page 103) or veggie broth

1 onion, roughly diced

1 bell pepper (any color), roughly diced

3 garlic cloves, minced

1 jalapeño, seeded, deribbed, and minced

2 teaspoons chili powder

1 teaspoon ground cumin

1 teaspoon salt

TOPPINGS: Grated Monterey Jack cheese, sour cream, cilantro, brown rice

This is officially my nine-year-old's new favorite soup! We ordered black bean soup at a restaurant years ago, and as soon as I saw how much she liked it I thought, I've got to come up with an easy way to make this at home. I hope your little ones enjoy this dish as much as mine do!

1. Combine all the ingredients in the slow cooker with 2 cups water. Cover and cook on high for 8 to 10 hours or overnight.

2. Blend until smooth with the immersion blender (or in the stand blender in batches). Serve warm with the desired toppings or store in the fridge or freezer.

LISA'S TIP: Some of my lovely recipe testers said they preferred this as a chunky soup rather than a smooth puree. You could certainly skip the last step if you prefer, or just blend half of it—this soup can easily go both ways, or anywhere in between!

Slow Cooker Chicken Tortilla Soup

One 28-ounce can stewed tomatoes (with juice), chopped

1 zucchini, trimmed and cut into 1-inch chunks

1 red bell pepper, seeded and cut into 1-inch chunks

1 onion, finely diced

1 cup frozen (no need to thaw) or fresh corn kernels

½ jalapeño, seeded and minced (or keep the seeds if you like it hot!)

3 garlic cloves, minced

1 tablespoon tomato paste

½ teaspoon dried oregano

1 teaspoon chili powder

1½ teaspoons ground cumin

½ teaspoon salt

1½ cups chicken broth, store bought or homemade (page 103)

1 to 1½ pounds boneless skinless chicken breasts (or thighs), trimmed and cut into 1- to 2-inch chunks

TOPPINGS: Grated Monterey Jack cheese, sour cream, cilantro leaves, sliced radishes, and/or corn tortillas, sliced into small triangles

This dish couldn't be any easier—and it's a crowd pleaser! This is the perfect weeknight recipe to come home to after a busy day at work or running around town. And if you're on a tight budget, feel free to substitute chicken thighs for the breasts so you can get more bang for your buck.

Difficulty: Easy
Prep time: Less than 20 minutes
Cook time: 4 to 5 hours on high or
    7 to 8 hours on low (hands off)
Makes 4 or 5 servings
Special tools needed: 6- or 7-quart slow cooker

GLUTEN-FREE
DAIRY-FREE
NUT-FREE
FREEZER-FRIENDLY

Combine all the ingredients in the slow cooker. Cover and cook on high for 4 to 5 hours or on low for 7 to 8 hours. Serve with the desired toppings. Store leftovers in the fridge for up to 5 days or the freezer for up to 6 months.

"I love using my slow cooker on busy weeknights!"

Easy Slow Cooker Steak Chili

With this chili recipe, my goal was to make things as quick and easy as possible. And trust me, it doesn't get much easier or more delicious than this one. This is my go-to meal for new moms or friends in need. I like to bring it over in freezer-proof jars so they have the option to either reheat it as needed (for dinner or lunch) or stick it in the freezer for another day!

1. Put the stew beef chunks in the bottom of the slow cooker. Sprinkle with the chili powder, cumin, salt, and cayenne. Top with the onion, beans, and tomatoes.

2. Cover and cook on high for 5 to 6 hours, until the beef is completely tender. Shred the beef with a fork before serving, if desired. Serve warm with the desired toppings.

> **LISA'S TIP:** When freezing soup in jars, be sure to leave room at the top for the liquid to expand.

Difficulty: Super easy

Prep time: 5 to 10 minutes

Cook time: 5 to 6 hours on high (hands off)

Makes 5 or 6 servings

Special tools needed: 6- or 7-quart slow cooker

GLUTEN-FREE
DAIRY-FREE (IF CHEESE AND SOUR CREAM ARE NOT USED AS TOPPINGS)
NUT-FREE
FREEZER-FRIENDLY

1½ pounds stew beef (grass-fed recommended), cut into 2-inch chunks

1 tablespoon chili powder

1 teaspoon ground cumin

1 teaspoon salt

⅛ teaspoon cayenne pepper (double this if you like it hot!)

½ onion, diced

One 15-ounce can kidney beans, drained and rinsed

One 28-ounce can diced tomatoes (with juice)

TOPPINGS: Grated Monterey Jack or Cheddar cheese, sour cream, diced avocado, and/or fresh cilantro

Gazpacho with Avocado and Crab

Gazpacho is such a refreshing cold soup to enjoy on hot summer days! I especially love this version with lump crabmeat on top for an extra special treat.

Roughly chop the tomatoes, cucumbers, bell peppers, and jalapeño into 3 or 4 big chunks. Toss them into the blender with the rest of the ingredients and blend just until smooth. Serve cold or at room temperature with the desired toppings.

Difficulty: Easy
Prep time: 15 to 20 minutes
Cook time: N/A
Makes 4 or 5 servings
Special tools needed: Blender

GLUTEN-FREE
DAIRY-FREE
NUT-FREE

2 tomatoes, cored

1 small cucumber, trimmed

1 red bell pepper, cored and seeded

⅓ cup cilantro leaves

½ jalapeño, seeded and deribbed (or keep the seeds, depending how much of a kick you want!)

2 green onions, white and green parts

1 garlic clove, smashed

2 tablespoons olive oil

1 tablespoon red wine vinegar

½ teaspoon salt

Ground black pepper

TOPPINGS: Avocado, lump crabmeat, and additional cilantro or green onions

simple dinners

simple dinner recipes

Black Bean Bowls

This recipe is the epitome of easy—it's almost like a deconstructed burrito! It's also allergy-friendly if you need something to serve to a variety of eaters.

In a medium bowl, combine the black beans, cilantro, green onions, lime juice, cumin, salt, chili powder, and cayenne and stir well. (The black bean mixture can be heated if you prefer it that way.) Serve over cooked rice and, if desired, top with sour cream.

> **LISA'S TIP:** Brown rice can take a while to cook, so I like to have a few store-bought bags of the precooked, microwavable kind on hand—just in case!

Difficulty: Super easy
Prep time: 5 to 10 minutes
Cook time: N/A
Makes 4 servings

GLUTEN-FREE
DAIRY-FREE (IF SOUR CREAM IS
    NOT USED)
VEGETARIAN
NUT-FREE

Two 15-ounce cans black beans, drained and rinsed

1 cup fresh cilantro leaves, chopped

4 green onions, white and green parts, chopped

Juice of 2 limes

1 teaspoon ground cumin

1 teaspoon salt

½ teaspoon chili powder

Big pinch cayenne pepper

Cooked brown rice, for serving

Sour cream (optional), for serving

Homemade Fish Sticks

Difficulty: Easy
Prep time: Less than 20 minutes
Cook time: 5 to 10 minutes
Makes 3 or 4 servings

DAIRY-FREE (IF OLIVE OIL IS USED
AND SAUCE IS OMITTED)
NUT-FREE
FREEZER-FRIENDLY

DIPPING SAUCE

½ cup sour cream

¼ cup chopped pickles
(or relish)

2 teaspoons fresh lemon juice

½ teaspoon mustard powder

FISH STICKS

¾ cup whole wheat
breadcrumbs

¼ cup whole wheat flour

1 egg

1 pound mild white fish (such as
cod, flounder, or rockfish), cut
into 2-inch-wide strips

Olive oil or ghee (clarified
butter)

Salt and ground black pepper

1 lemon, halved

Fish sticks are incredibly easy to make and soooo much better tasting (and better for you!) than the store-bought version. You can control the ingredients, including fresh, wild-caught fish, whole-grain breading, and organic oil. Use the same method to make chicken nuggets and you have two dinners nailed for the week.

1. To make the dipping sauce: In a small bowl, combine the sour cream, pickles, lemon juice, and mustard powder. Set aside.

2. To make the fish sticks: In a medium bowl, combine the breadcrumbs and flour. In another medium bowl, beat the egg with a splash of water.

3. Designate one hand as your "wet hand" (for the egg) and one as your "dry hand" (for the breadcrumbs). Using your wet hand, pick up a fish strip, drop it into the egg bowl, and stir it around to coat. Let any excess egg drip off, then drop it onto the breadcrumb mixture. Using your dry hand, sprinkle breading on the top and sides until the fish is well coated. Transfer to a clean plate and repeat to bread the rest of the fish.

4. In a large sauté pan, heat a thin layer of the olive oil or ghee over medium heat. Add the fish to the pan in one layer (or hold some back if necessary to cook in a second batch). Cook until golden brown and cooked all the way through, 2 to 4 minutes per side (depending on the thickness of the fish). Season the fish with salt and pepper to taste and squeeze a lemon half over the fish. Slice the other half lemon into wedges and serve with the warm fish and dipping sauce on the side.

Creamy Mac and Peas

This is a popular dish at our house when we leave the kids home alone with a babysitter! Stirring in frozen peas at the end officially makes this a one-dish meal and also cools it down enough for little ones to start chowing down right away. If you aren't into peas, diced fresh tomato is a fabulous substitute!

1. Cook the noodles according to package directions, drain, and set aside.

2. In the pot you used to boil the noodles, melt the butter over medium-low heat. Stir in ⅔ cup of the cream until well combined.

3. Reduce the heat to low and add the macaroni, cheese, and salt. Cook, stirring, until the cheese melts. Stir in the remaining 2 tablespoons cream at the end. Mix in the frozen peas, season with black pepper to taste, and serve immediately.

"This is our go-to meal for the babysitter and the kids when we're going out!"

Difficulty: Super easy
Prep time: 5 to 10 minutes
Cook time: 10 to 15 minutes
Makes 4 or 5 servings

**GLUTEN-FREE (IF GLUTEN-FREE
NOODLES ARE USED)**
VEGETARIAN
NUT-FREE

3 cups uncooked whole wheat elbow macaroni

4 tablespoons (½ stick) butter

⅔ cup plus 2 tablespoons heavy cream

2½ cups freshly grated cheese (Cheddar, Monterey Jack, or a combo, along with some Parmesan!)

½ teaspoon salt

½ cup frozen peas (no need to thaw)

Ground black pepper

Crispy Pork with a Cracker Crust

Difficulty: Easy

Prep time: 10 minutes

Cook time: 10 minutes

Makes 4 servings

Special tools needed: Food processor

GLUTEN-FREE (IF GLUTEN-FREE CRACKERS ARE USED)

DAIRY-FREE (IF PARMESAN GARNISH IS OMITTED)

NUT-FREE

14 whole-grain woven wheat crackers (such as Triscuit or Back to Nature)

½ teaspoon paprika

½ teaspoon garlic powder

½ teaspoon onion powder

½ teaspoon dried thyme

¼ teaspoon salt

¼ teaspoon ground black pepper

4 boneless pork chops, about ¾ inch thick

3 to 4 tablespoons olive oil

GARNISH (OPTIONAL):
Freshly grated Parmesan cheese or honey-mustard sauce (mix together equal parts honey and mustard)

It's hard to go wrong with a crispy crust and this pork recipe is no exception! Pair with a simple green salad and Sydney's Roasted Potatoes (page 151) and you have yourself a wholesome weeknight dinner that your family will gobble up in no time.

1. In the food processor, pulse together the crackers and seasonings (all the way down to the pepper) until crumbly. Spread on a large plate and set aside.

2. Coat both sides of the pork chops with 2 tablespoons of the olive oil. It helps to throw it all in a big plastic bag together and toss it around.

3. Press the pork chops into the cracker mixture until well coated on all sides.

4. In a large skillet, heat 1 tablespoon of the olive oil over medium heat. Add the pork chops and cook until golden brown on both sides and no longer pink in the center, 3 to 4 minutes per side. Add another tablespoon of oil to the pan if it begins to dry out.

5. Serve, topped with one of the garnishes, if desired.

Veggie and Bean Burritos with Cilantro-Lime Crema

FILLING

1 tablespoon olive oil

1 onion, halved and thinly sliced

1 bell pepper (any color), cut into strips

½ jalapeño, seeded and minced (save the other half to serve on the side if you like it spicy!)

One 15-ounce can black or pinto beans, drained and rinsed

2 garlic cloves, minced

¾ teaspoon chili powder

¾ teaspoon ground cumin

¾ teaspoon salt

CILANTRO-LIME CREMA

⅔ cup sour cream

⅓ cup fresh cilantro, chopped

2 tablespoons fresh lime juice (about 1 lime)

ASSEMBLY

Six 8- or 10-inch whole wheat flour tortillas (homemade or good-quality store-bought)

1½ cups freshly shredded Monterey Jack cheese

We love to throw some vegetarian dinners in the mix each week, and this one is a family favorite. It's so filling and satisfying that even your biggest meat lovers won't notice anything is missing!

Difficulty: Easy
Prep time: 10 to 15 minutes
Cook time: 10 to 15 minutes
Makes 4 or 5 servings

GLUTEN-FREE (IF GLUTEN-FREE TORTILLAS ARE USED)
VEGETARIAN
NUT-FREE
FREEZER-FRIENDLY

1. To make the filling: In a large sauté pan, heat the olive oil over medium heat. Add the onion and cook, stirring occasionally, until the onion begins to soften and brown, 3 to 4 minutes. Throw in the bell pepper and jalapeño and sauté until the veggies can easily be pierced with a fork, 5 minutes or so.

2. Add the beans, garlic, and seasonings and cook until the beans are heated through, another 1 or 2 minutes.

3. Meanwhile, to make the cilantro-lime crema: In a small bowl, whisk together the sour cream, cilantro, and lime juice.

4. To assemble the burritos: Lay out the tortillas on plates or foil. Evenly distribute the Monterey Jack and then the veggie filling in a strip down the middle. Fold up the burritos on the bottom and then the sides and roll them up. Serve warm with the crema as a dipping sauce.

> **LISA'S TIP:** We sometimes wrap these in foil and bring them with us camping. All you have to do is place them in (or around) the campfire to briefly heat them up!

Lamb Burgers

Swapping out the usual ground beef for lamb in your burgers is a super easy way to get out of your dinner rut! We love lamb at our house, but if you aren't sure what your family will think, try using half lamb and half beef to ease them into the idea. Good luck!

1. Preheat the gas grill to 425°F (or prepare a charcoal fire).

2. In a medium bowl, use your hands to mix together the meat, mint, parsley, garlic, cumin, salt, and pepper to taste. Form the mixture into 4 patties and press down on the centers to help keep the burgers flat on the grill.

3. Grill the burgers for a total of 15 to 20 minutes, flipping them over halfway through. The USDA recommends cooking ground meat to a minimum internal temperature of 160°F. (Note: They will shrink in size some during cooking.)

4. Cut the burgers in half, place them inside the pockets of the halved pitas, top with the Tzatziki Sauce, and serve.

> **LISA'S TIP:** To really make this dish extra special, brown the pitas in a little butter in a skillet over medium heat for a minute or two so they can be served warm.

Difficulty: Easy
Prep time: 10 to 15 minutes
Cook time: 15 to 20 minutes
Makes 4 servings
Special tools needed:
  Outdoor grill

GLUTEN-FREE (IF GLUTEN-FREE PITAS OR BREAD ARE USED)
DAIRY-FREE
NUT-FREE
FREEZER-FRIENDLY

1 pound ground lamb

½ cup fresh mint leaves, chopped

¼ cup fresh parsley leaves, chopped

2 garlic cloves, minced

1 teaspoon ground cumin

½ teaspoon salt

Ground black pepper

4 whole wheat pitas, halved, for serving

Tzatziki Sauce (page 275), for serving

Parmesan-Crusted Chicken

This very simple dish is packed with great flavor. It's a good way to switch up other-wise boring chicken breasts. Serve with a big green salad (such as the Simple Salad Mix on page 125) and "Rice" Pilaf (page 135) and you'll be good to go!

1. Trim the fat off the chicken, cut it into 4 equal pieces, pound both sides with the meat tenderizer (I like to cover it with plastic wrap first to prevent splattering), season with salt and pepper, and set aside.

2. Lightly beat the egg in a shallow bowl. On a plate, combine the breadcrumbs and Parmesan and mix with a fork. Set aside a large clean plate for the chicken.

3. Designate one hand as your "wet hand" (for the egg) and one as your "dry hand" (for the breadcrumbs). Using your wet hand, coat a piece of chicken in the egg mixture, then drop it on top of the bread-crumb mixture. Using your dry hand, sprinkle some breadcrumbs on top of the chicken and flip over a few times, to coat it evenly. Place it on the plate and repeat to bread the rest of the chicken.

4. In a large sauté pan, melt a thin layer of butter (1 to 2 tablespoons, depending on the size of your pan) over medium-low heat. Add the chicken and cook (in batches, if necessary) until golden brown on both sides and cooked all the way through, 5 to 7 minutes on each side (turn the chicken very gently so as not to disturb the crust). Cut a piece down the middle to make sure it is fully cooked (no longer pink inside) and transfer to a plate lined with paper towels.

5. With the pan still over medium heat, melt another tablespoon butter. Add the shallot and cook until softened, 2 to 3 minutes. Pour in the wine and increase the heat to high. Cook for several minutes to reduce by half, then pour in the lemon juice and stir to combine.

6. Drizzle the sauce over the chicken, sprinkle with the parsley, and serve.

Difficulty: Easy
Prep time: 15 to 20 minutes
Cook time: 15 minutes
Makes 4 servings
Special tools needed: Meat tenderizer

GLUTEN-FREE (IF GLUTEN-FREE BREADCRUMBS ARE USED)
NUT-FREE

1 pound boneless, skinless chicken breasts

Salt and ground black pepper

1 egg

⅔ cup whole wheat breadcrumbs

⅓ cup finely grated Parmesan cheese

Butter, for cooking

1 shallot, minced

½ cup white wine

2 tablespoons fresh lemon juice

Handful of fresh parsley, chopped

Easy Fish Tacos with Pico de Gallo

Difficulty: Easy
Prep time: 15 to 20 minutes
Cook time: 8 to 10 minutes
Makes 4 or 5 servings

DAIRY-FREE (IF OLIVE OIL IS USED INSTEAD OF BUTTER)
NUT-FREE

PICO DE GALLO

1 medium tomato (about ½ pound), seeded and diced

½ cup diced white onion

½ serrano or jalapeño pepper, seeded and minced

¼ cup chopped fresh cilantro

1 tablespoon fresh lime juice

Pinch of salt

FISH

½ cup whole wheat flour

1½ teaspoons chili powder

½ teaspoon ground cumin

½ teaspoon salt

⅛ teaspoon cayenne pepper

1 pound white fish (such as cod, rockfish, or tilapia), cut into 1- to 2-inch chunks

2 to 3 tablespoons butter or olive oil

1 lime, halved

Warm whole-grain corn or flour tortillas, for serving

For years I claimed I did not like fish tacos, but I'm here to report that I've come to my senses. This is one of my husband's favorite dishes, so little by little (bite by bite of his) I warmed up to the idea. Now I'm excited to share this super easy version that's quick enough to throw together on any busy weeknight!

1. Make the pico de gallo: In a medium bowl, toss together all the ingredients.

2. Prepare the fish: Mix the flour and seasonings on a plate. Dip the fish chunks into the flour to coat on all sides. Transfer to a clean plate.

3. In a large sauté pan, melt the butter over medium heat. Add the fish and cook until the fish is golden brown on the bottom, 3 to 4 minutes (depending on the thickness of the fish). Flip and cook until it is golden brown on the other side and the center is white, flaky, and cooked all the way through, 7 to 8 minutes total (depending on the thickness). Add more butter to the pan if necessary to keep it from drying out. Squeeze the lime on top.

4. Serve the fish with warm tortillas and freshly made pico de gallo.

Roasted Summer Vegetable Pasta

1 eggplant (12 to 13 ounces), cut into 1-inch cubes

2 medium zucchini or other summer squash (7 to 8 ounces each), cut into 1-inch cubes

2 Roma (plum) tomatoes (optional), cut into 1-inch chunks and stems removed

2 garlic cloves, minced

⅓ cup dry white wine

3 tablespoons olive oil

1¼ teaspoons dried thyme

1½ teaspoons salt (or less, if the tomato sauce has salt added)

Ground black pepper

8 ounces uncooked whole-grain noodles, cooked according to the package directions

One 15-ounce can (or jar) unseasoned tomato sauce (preferably no-salt-added)

¾ cup freshly grated Parmesan cheese

This recipe was inspired by one of our favorite meals we had on a trip to France. And it wasn't at an uppity, expensive restaurant in Paris . . . just at a little road-side café in the small town of Cluny at the über-reasonable cost of 8 euros (about 10 bucks).

Difficulty: Easy
Prep time: 10 minutes
Cook time: 45 minutes (mostly hands off)
Makes 5 or 6 servings
Special tools needed: 9 x 13-inch baking dish

GLUTEN-FREE (IF GLUTEN-FREE NOODLES ARE USED)
VEGETARIAN
NUT-FREE

1. Preheat the oven to 425°F.

2. In the baking dish, combine the eggplant, zucchini, tomatoes (if using), and garlic. Add the wine, olive oil, and seasonings and toss to combine. Roast until the veggies are tender and brown, about 40 minutes, stirring once halfway through the cooking time.

3. Stir the noodles and tomato sauce into the veggies. Top with the Parmesan and stick the casserole back in the oven until the cheese is melted, about 5 minutes. Serve warm and enjoy!

Real-Food Sloppy Joes!

One day my poor daughter said to me, "Mommy, I keep reading all these books that talk about Sloppy Joes, and I've never had one before. Can you please make some so I can finally try it like everyone else?" Gosh, she is so deprived! Seriously, though, if that's her biggest problem any given week, I'll gladly take it. Not to mention it was a "problem" easily solved with this recipe, which I hope your family enjoys as much as mine did.

1. In a sauté pan, heat the oil over medium heat. Add the onion, celery, and carrot and cook until they begin to soften but not brown, 2 to 3 minutes.

2. Add the beef and garlic and cook, breaking up the meat with a spatula, until the meat has browned all the way through, 5 to 6 minutes. Season with the salt and pepper. Drain off and discard the fat.

3. Add the tomato sauce, honey, mustard, vinegar, chili powder, and cinnamon and simmer over low heat until the sauce thickens, 10 to 15 minutes.

4. Serve warm with whole wheat buns and some yummy vegetables such as Brussels sprouts (page 140), zucchini (page 144), or coleslaw (pages 131 and 132) on the side.

Difficulty: Easy
Prep time: Less than 10 minutes
Cook time: 20 minutes
Makes 4 or 5 servings

GLUTEN-FREE (IF GLUTEN-FREE
  BUNS ARE USED)
DAIRY-FREE
NUT-FREE
FREEZER-FRIENDLY

1 tablespoon olive oil

½ cup diced onion

1 celery stalk, diced

1 carrot, peeled and diced

1 pound ground beef

1 garlic clove, minced

½ teaspoon salt

A couple dashes of ground
black pepper

One 15-ounce can unseasoned
tomato sauce

1 tablespoon honey

1 teaspoon yellow mustard

1 teaspoon apple cider vinegar

1½ teaspoons chili powder

Pinch of ground cinnamon

Toasted whole wheat buns,
for serving (use small buns or
dinner rolls for sliders!)

Simple Salmon with Pinot Noir

Difficulty: Super easy
Prep time: 5 minutes
Cook time: 10 to 15 minutes
Makes 4 servings

NUT-FREE

½ cup whole wheat flour

1 pound wild-caught salmon
(I like mine with the skin
off—the butcher will do it if
you ask)

Salt and ground black pepper

2 tablespoons butter (or more
as needed)

½ cup Pinot Noir

Thyme sprigs, for garnish
(optional)

Pinot Noir is a super easy way to transform your salmon dinner. I'm honestly not always a huge fan of salmon (I usually prefer milder fish), but this recipe is one way I'll happily scarf it down! My kids love it, too, wine sauce and all (don't worry, the alcohol gets cooked off).

1. Sprinkle the flour onto a large plate. Season the fish with salt and pepper and then dip it in the flour to coat on all sides. Transfer to a clean plate.

2. In a large skillet, melt the butter over medium heat. Add the fish and cook until golden brown on the bottom, 3 to 4 minutes (depending on the thickness of the fish). Flip and cook until it is golden brown on the other side and the center is flaky and cooked all the way through, 2 to 3 minutes. Add more butter if the fish has soaked it all up and the pan looks dry. Transfer the fish to a clean plate and cover it with foil to keep warm.

3. To make the sauce, add the wine to the pan and increase the heat to high. Cook the wine until reduced by half, 3 to 4 minutes, at the same time scraping the browned bits off the bottom of the pan and incorporating them into the sauce.

4. Drizzle the sauce over the fish and serve warm. Add more salt to taste and garnish with thyme sprigs, if desired.

> **LISA'S TIP:** Several of my recipe testers said they aren't normally salmon fans either, but that this recipe won them over. So even if you're skeptical (like us!), give this one a try to see if it will change your mind.

Arugula-Walnut Pesto Pasta with Zucchini

This quick weeknight meal helps you easily up your veggie consumption for the day. My kids even like this one cold in their lunch box (when it's more like a pasta salad), so if you're in the mood, double the recipe so you can have leftovers!

1. To make the pesto: In the blender or food processor, combine all the ingredients and puree until smooth. Set aside.

2. To cook the pasta: In a large pot of boiling water, cook the pasta according to the package directions and with only 4 to 5 minutes remaining, drop the zucchini into the boiling water with the pasta. Drain when done and return the pasta and zucchini to the pot.

3. Add the pesto to the pot and toss to combine. Spoon into pasta bowls and serve topped with the extra Parmesan.

Difficulty: Easy
Prep time: 10 minutes
Cook time: 10 to 15 minutes
Makes 3 or 4 servings
Special tools needed: Blender or food processor

GLUTEN-FREE (IF GLUTEN-FREE PASTA IS USED)
VEGETARIAN

PESTO

1½ cups loosely packed arugula leaves (about 2 ounces)

1½ cups parsley leaves

½ cup walnuts

½ cup freshly grated Parmesan cheese

⅓ cup plus 1 tablespoon olive oil

2 tablespoons fresh lemon juice

1 garlic clove, minced

½ teaspoon salt

PASTA

8 ounces uncooked penne or fusilli

2 zucchini, trimmed, halved lengthwise, and cut crosswise into ¼-inch-thick half-moons

Extra grated Parmesan cheese, for serving

Simple Roasted Pork Tenderloin

Difficulty: Super easy
Prep time: 5 minutes
Cook time: 25 to 30 minutes
(depending on the size
of the tenderloin)
Makes 4 servings
Special tools needed: Small
baking dish

GLUTEN-FREE
DAIRY-FREE
NUT-FREE
FREEZER-FRIENDLY

One 1- to 1½-pound pork
tenderloin (not to be
confused with pork loin)

1 teaspoon paprika

½ teaspoon garlic powder

½ teaspoon onion powder

½ teaspoon salt

⅛ teaspoon ground black
pepper

1 tablespoon olive oil

This is the epitome of a super simple weeknight meal. Throw together some quick side dishes (such as the "Rice" Pilaf on page 135 and some steamed broccoli) while it's roasting and you'll have a satisfying weeknight meal on the table in no time!

1. Preheat the oven to 425°F.

2. Place the pork in the small square or round baking dish (curl it up if necessary to make it fit).

3. In a small bowl, combine the seasonings and stir in the olive oil to make a paste. Brush half the paste over the top of the pork, then turn it over and repeat.

4. Bake until the pork is cooked all the way through (no longer pink and to an internal temperature of 160°F), 25 to 35 minutes, depending on the size. Slice and serve warm.

Weeknight Mushroom and Kale Pasta

When this simple pasta is on the menu, my younger daughter will yell from upstairs, "Mommy, what are you making?!? It smells sooooo good down there!" That girl has come to love good food, and I love to make it, which makes us a perfect match.

1. In a small saucepan, combine the dried mushrooms and 1½ cups water. Bring to a boil over high heat, then reduce to a simmer and cook until the mushrooms have softened, 3 to 4 minutes. Reserving the cooking liquid, drain the mushrooms in a fine-mesh sieve. Measure the cooking liquid and if it's less than 1 cup, add some water. Dice the mushrooms and set aside.

2. In a large sauté pan, melt the butter over medium heat. Add the mushrooms, shallots, and garlic and cook, stirring, until the shallots begin to soften, 2 to 3 minutes.

3. Pour in the wine, increase the heat, and bring the mixture to a boil. Cook until the wine almost completely boils off and is reduced down to a couple tablespoons, 3 to 4 minutes (if you are doubling this recipe, it will take longer).

4. Pour in the reserved mushroom cooking liquid and cook for several minutes until reduced by half. Reduce the heat to medium and add the cream, kale, salt, and pepper to taste. Cook until the sauce thickens, 2 to 3 more minutes.

5. Fold in the pasta and serve garnished with the Parmesan.

> **LISA'S TIP:** If you aren't into dried mushrooms, some blog readers have told me they've made this recipe with fresh mushrooms and used broth in place of the cooking liquid and that it turned out great!

Difficulty: Easy
Prep time: 5 to 10 minutes
Cook time: About 20 minutes
Makes 3 or 4 servings

GLUTEN-FREE (IF GLUTEN-FREE PASTA IS USED)
VEGETARIAN
NUT-FREE

1 ounce dried wild mushrooms, such as porcini or shiitake

2 tablespoons butter

2 shallots, diced

3 garlic cloves, minced

½ cup dry white wine

¾ cup heavy cream

3 cups loosely packed kale (thick ribs removed, leaves cut into strips)

½ teaspoon salt

Ground black pepper

8 ounces uncooked whole wheat pasta (such as penne), cooked according to the package directions

⅓ cup freshly grated Parmesan cheese

Small-Batch Shrimp Boil

Difficulty: Super easy
Prep time: 5 to 10 minutes
Cook time: 10 minutes
**Seasonal note: Use locally
grown corn in the summer
months.**
Makes 4 or 5 servings

GLUTEN-FREE
DAIRY-FREE
NUT-FREE

**2 tablespoons Old Bay
seasoning**

1 teaspoon salt

**¾ pound red potatoes, cut
into 1-inch pieces**

**½ onion, cut into 6 wedges
and separated**

**½ pound smoked sausage,
cut into 1-inch chunks**

**3 ears corn, husked and cut
into thirds**

**1 pound large shrimp, peels
left on**

Traditionally a Southern shrimp boil is saved for special occasions and big crowds. And while it's great for any big event, it can also be a super quick and easy weeknight dinner when pared down to reasonable quantities. I'm excited to share this small-batch version, which can be whipped up in no time without sacrificing any of the flavor or fun!

1. Fill a large pot with 10 cups of water, whisk in the Old Bay seasoning and salt, and bring to a boil over high heat.

2. Add the potatoes and onion and boil for 5 minutes. Throw in the sausage, corn, and shrimp and bring back to a boil. Cook until the shrimp are pink and cooked through, about 5 minutes. Drain the liquid (and discard).

"This is a popular combo where we live in the South!"

Taco Stuffed Peppers

This is such a fun and fancy makeover of a family favorite . . . tacos! We're huge fans of Mexican food any day of the week, and my daughters were super excited when I served our beloved taco recipe in their own individual bell pepper "bowls" instead of the standard tortillas. I even sent the leftovers cold to school the next day (along with Thermoses of warm Slow Cooker Black Bean Soup, page 192), and it was a huge hit with both of them. Score!

1. Preheat the oven to 400°F.

2. Halve the bell peppers lengthwise. Scoop the cores and seeds out of the middle and discard. Place the peppers in the baking dish with the cut sides facing up and bake until tender when pierced by a fork, 15 to 20 minutes.

3. Meanwhile, in a large sauté pan, heat the oil over medium heat. Add the onion and cook until soft but not browned, 3 to 4 minutes.

4. Add the meat and cook until browned and cooked through, 5 to 6 minutes, breaking it up with a spatula. Drain off the fat, then season the meat with the chili powder, cumin, oregano, salt, and lime juice.

5. Pull the peppers out of the oven and turn on the broiler. If liquid has accumulated in the cooked peppers, use tongs to drain them into the sink. Divide the taco filling evenly among the pepper cavities. Sprinkle with the cheese and broil the stuffed peppers until the cheese on top turns golden brown, 3 to 5 minutes. Take care that it doesn't burn; the broiler works quickly! Serve warm topped with sour cream and cilantro, if desired.

> **LISA'S TIP:** You could also make this dish with only ½ pound of meat and add a can of drained black or pinto beans.

Difficulty: Easy
Prep time: 5 minutes
Cook time: 20 to 25 minutes
Makes 4 servings
Special tools needed: 9 x 13-inch baking dish

GLUTEN-FREE
DAIRY-FREE (OMIT THE CHEESE AND SOUR CREAM TOPPING)
NUT-FREE
FREEZER-FRIENDLY

4 large bell peppers, any color

2 tablespoons olive oil

½ onion

1 pound ground pork or beef

1 teaspoon chili powder

½ teaspoon ground cumin

½ teaspoon dried oregano

½ teaspoon salt

Juice of 1 lime

1 cup freshly grated Monterey Jack or pepper Jack cheese

TOPPINGS: Sour cream and cilantro

Butternut Squash Pasta with Sage Brown Butter Sauce

Difficulty: Medium
Prep time: 5 to 10 minutes
Cook time: 30 minutes
Makes 5 or 6 servings
Special tools needed: Rimmed
  baking sheet

GLUTEN-FREE (IF GLUTEN-FREE
  PASTA IS USED)
VEGETARIAN
NUT-FREE

Two 14-ounce packages cubed
butternut squash (or a 2¼- to
2½-pound butternut squash,
peeled and cut into 1-inch
cubes, although this will add
some time to the preparation)

1 tablespoon olive oil

Salt and ground black pepper

12 ounces uncooked whole
wheat spaghetti or angel hair
pasta

¾ cup fresh sage leaves (about
a 0.75-ounce pack)

1 stick (4 ounces) butter

¾ cup freshly grated Parmesan
cheese

I love homemade butternut squash ravioli with a brown butter sage sauce so much that I had to come up with an easy "deconstructed" version. While homemade ravioli is always a fun kitchen project, it's not every day (or even every month) we have time to take something like this on. So I'm thankful to have this super quick and easy version to do the trick in the meantime!

1. Preheat the oven to 400°F.

2. On the rimmed baking sheet, toss the squash cubes with the olive oil and a little salt and pepper. Roast until tender when pierced with a fork, 25 to 30 minutes.

3. In a large pot of boiling water, cook the pasta according to the package directions. Drain and set aside.

4. Remove the sage leaves from the stems, wash, and pat them dry to ensure that they brown in the pan.

5. In a medium skillet, melt the butter over medium heat. Add the sage leaves, and cook, stirring occasionally, until the butter just begins to brown (but does not burn). Watch closely because it can go from brown to burned very quickly. Remove from the heat and set aside.

6. To serve, spoon the pasta into large bowls, top with the roasted squash, butter-sage sauce, Parmesan, and salt and pepper to taste.

Slow Cooker Shredded Pork and Bean Tacos

1 onion, peeled and quartered

One 2½- to 3-pound boneless pork shoulder roast

1 tablespoon chili powder

2 teaspoons paprika

1½ teaspoons ground cumin

1½ teaspoons dried oregano

1½ teaspoons salt

½ teaspoon ground black pepper

½ to 1 jalapeño, diced (depending on how much heat you like!)

Two 15-ounce cans black and/or pinto beans, drained and rinsed

FOR SERVING:

Whole-grain flour or corn tortillas

Shredded Monterey Jack cheese

Lime and Cilantro Coleslaw (page 132)

Sliced avocado

This is my new favorite slow cooker dish, and the best part is that it feeds a crowd or (if you don't happen to have a crowd) makes great leftovers. Be sure to serve it with the Lime and Cilantro Coleslaw (page 132)!

Difficulty: Super easy
Prep time: 10 to 15 minutes
Cook time: 7 to 8 hours on low (hands off)
Makes 6 to 8 servings
Special tools needed: 6- or 7-quart slow cooker

GLUTEN-FREE (IF CORN TORTILLAS ARE USED)
DAIRY-FREE (IF CHEESE AND COLESLAW TOPPINGS ARE
    NOT USED)
NUT-FREE
FREEZER-FRIENDLY (AFTER THE MEAT IS COOKED)

1. Place the onion in the slow cooker. Put the pork shoulder on top.

2. In a small bowl, mix the chili powder, paprika, cumin, oregano, salt, and pepper. Sprinkle half the seasoning mixture on top of the pork, flip it over, and sprinkle the rest on top.

3. Scatter the jalapeño on top of the pork, then pour the beans around the base of the meat. Cover and cook on low for 7 to 8 hours, until the pork is easily shredded with a fork.

4. To serve, place the meat on a cutting board and use two forks to shred it into a serving bowl. Use a slotted spoon to retrieve the beans, then mix them into the shredded meat. Pour a few spoonfuls of the cooking liquid on top.

5. Serve with tortillas, cheese, coleslaw, and avocado.

Weeknight Beef Bourguignon

This is one of our all-time favorite slow cooker recipes! Beef bourguignon is normally a pretty labor-intensive dish, but I figured out how to cut and combine enough steps to make this an easy weeknight meal by adapting a recipe from TheKitchn.com. The result is the epitome of comfort food.

1. In your largest skillet, cook the bacon over medium heat until browned and crispy. Drain on paper towels. Reserving the bacon grease, pour off all but 1 tablespoon of it from the skillet. Crumble the cooked bacon into the bottom of the slow cooker.

2. Return the skillet to medium-high heat. Working in batches if necessary, sear the cubed beef for a few minutes until golden brown on the top and bottom (make sure the pieces have enough room for a good sear). Add to the slow cooker.

3. Deglaze the skillet by adding the wine and turning the heat to high while scraping the browned bits off the bottom of the pan. Cook until the liquid is reduced by half, 3 to 4 minutes, then pour into the slow cooker.

4. Add 1 tablespoon of the reserved bacon grease (or olive oil) to the skillet, increase the heat to medium, add the diced veggies, and cook, stirring occasionally, until softened, 2 to 3 minutes. Add the veggies to the slow cooker with the salt, thyme, and broth. Cover and cook on low for 6 to 8 hours.

5. Serve over whole-grain noodles and enjoy.

LISA'S TIP: For a real treat, make gravy (page 279) with the broth when the dish is done cooking. I highly recommend it!

Difficulty: Medium

Prep time: Less than 20 minutes

Cook time: 6 to 8 hours on low (hands off)

Makes 5 or 6 servings

Special tools needed: 6- or 7-quart slow cooker

GLUTEN-FREE
DAIRY-FREE
NUT-FREE
FREEZER-FRIENDLY

4 slices bacon

2½ pounds cubed beef stew meat

2 cups dry red wine, such as Merlot

1 onion, finely diced

3 or 4 carrots, peeled and cut into large dice

3 or 4 celery stalks, trimmed and cut into large dice

1 teaspoon salt

½ teaspoon dried thyme (or leaves from 2 to 3 fresh thyme sprigs)

2 to 3 cups chicken (page 103), beef, or veggie broth—just enough to cover the meat

Cooked whole-grain noodles, for serving

CHAPTER 9

special treats

special treat recipes

Cinnamon-Glazed Bananas

This dessert is similar to Bananas Foster. It's fabulous by itself and even better over vanilla ice cream. Such a tasty real-food treat!

In a skillet, combine the butter, maple syrup, cinnamon, and vanilla and set over medium heat. When it starts bubbling, add the bananas and cook for 30 to 60 seconds, stirring to coat. Serve as is or over vanilla ice cream.

> **LISA'S TIP:** You could try this cooking method with other fruits as well, such as apples, pears, or blueberries!

"You should totally put this recipe in your new cookbook—it's my new favorite dessert!"

—SIENNA LEAKE, AGE 9

Difficulty: Super easy
Prep time: 5 minutes
Cook time: 5 minutes
Makes 4 or 5 servings

GLUTEN-FREE
DAIRY-FREE (IF COCONUT OIL IS
   SUBSTITUTED FOR THE BUTTER)
VEGETARIAN
NUT-FREE

2 tablespoons butter

¼ cup pure maple syrup

½ teaspoon ground cinnamon

1 teaspoon pure vanilla extract

4 large bananas, cut into
½-inch-thick slices

Vanilla ice cream (optional),
for serving

Homemade Dark Chocolate Fudge Pops

Difficulty: Super easy
Prep time: Less than 10 minutes
Freeze time: 4 to 5 hours
Makes ten 2-ounce ice pops
Special tools needed: Ice pop molds with sticks

GLUTEN-FREE
VEGETARIAN
NUT-FREE
FREEZER-FRIENDLY

⅔ cup pure maple syrup

½ cup unsweetened cocoa powder (I prefer the "special dark" 100% cacao variety)

2 teaspoons pure vanilla extract

1 cup plus 1 tablespoon plain yogurt

1¼ cups milk

I was a big fan of fudge pops when I was younger, so I'm excited to have this better-for-you homemade version to take me back to my childhood! Funnily enough, my daughter actually told me I was "acting like a kid" while we were eating them together for the first time. Oops, I must have gotten a little messy and proclaimed how good it was one too many times.

1. In a medium bowl, whisk together the maple syrup, cocoa, and vanilla until thoroughly combined, with almost no clumps. Slowly whisk in the yogurt and milk.

2. Divide the mixture among the ice pop molds, add the ice pop sticks, and freeze for at least 4 to 5 hours. When you're ready to dig in, run a little bit of warm water on the outside of the molds to loosen them up so the ice pops come out easily.

Mint Chocolate Truffles

My older daughter is a huge mint chocolate fan, so she was thrilled when I made this mint version of the chocolate truffles from my first cookbook. The first time she tried them she excitedly said, "These taste like candy canes!" I think that says it all about these fun little bite-size desserts that would be very appropriate during the holidays.

1. In the food processor, combine all the ingredients and blend. Add 1 to 2 tablespoons water if necessary to help the mixture stick together.

2. Remove the mixture from the machine and form it into one big piece on a baking sheet. Using your hands, divide it into a dozen pieces and roll each piece into a round little truffle. Serve or store in an airtight container in the refrigerator for up to 3 or 4 days.

Difficulty: Medium
Prep time: Less than 15 minutes
Cook time: N/A
Makes 12 truffles
Special tools needed: Food processor

GLUTEN-FREE
DAIRY-FREE
VEGETARIAN

1 cup pitted dates

1 cup raw almonds

2 tablespoons pure maple syrup

1 tablespoon unsweetened cocoa powder (I prefer the "special dark" 100% cacao variety)

¼ teaspoon peppermint extract

Chocolate Banana Pops

Difficulty: Easy
Prep time: 10 to 15 minutes
Freeze time: 3 to 4 hours
Makes 8 pops
Special tools needed: 8 ice pop
sticks, wax paper

GLUTEN-FREE
DAIRY-FREE
VEGETARIAN
NUT-FREE (IF TOPPINGS ARE
  OMITTED)
FREEZER-FRIENDLY

4 bananas (a firm banana is
better than overripe in this
recipe!)

2 ounces unsweetened baking
chocolate, broken into pieces

¼ cup pure maple syrup

OPTIONAL TOPPINGS:
Unsweetened shredded
coconut (plain or toasted) or
crushed roasted peanuts

The first time I made these, my older daughter asked me approximately twelve hundred times if she could have another one. Clearly she is a huge fan and I know your little ones will love them, too. Just be sure to ask them to help you make them—because that's the fun part!

1. Peel the bananas and halve them crosswise. Stick an ice pop stick into the flat (cut) part of each banana half and place them on a plate or cutting board lined with wax paper.

2. In a small saucepan, combine the chocolate and maple syrup and melt over low heat, stirring frequently. Remove immediately from the heat.

3. One by one, angle each banana half over the pot and slowly twirl it around in the chocolate while spooning more over the banana. Transfer to the prepared plate and sprinkle with a topping (if using). Repeat to make the rest of the pops. Freeze for at least 3 to 4 hours before serving.

LISA'S TIP: These would be great to serve at a children's party at home or at school (just be sure to omit the toppings if anyone has allergies).

Real-Food Snow Cones!

Making a real-food snow cone honestly couldn't be any easier. Think about it—a typical snow cone is basically just ice (that's definitely real) topped off with highly processed syrup (that's definitely not real—see Tip). There's just no need for all these unwanted additives and chemicals when you can simply pour an organic juice concentrate mixture over all that shaved ice instead!

1. Make the "syrup" by mixing the fruit juice concentrate with 3 tablespoons water.

2. "Shave" the ice by using the blender or snow cone machine. Arrange the shaved ice in the snow cone cups. If you like, use an ice cream scooper to achieve a nice rounded top. Dividing evenly, pour the homemade "syrup" over the top, insert a straw, and enjoy!

> **LISA'S TIP:** Typical snow cone syrup usually includes high fructose corn syrup, citric acid, artificial flavor, propylene glycol, sodium benzoate (preservative), sodium saccharin, xanthan gum, and artificial food dye. As usual, homemade is better!

Difficulty: Super easy
Prep time: 5 to 10 minutes
Cook time: N/A
Makes 6 servings
Special tools needed: Blender or snow cone machine, snow cone cups, and straws

GLUTEN-FREE
DAIRY-FREE
VEGETARIAN
NUT-FREE

6 tablespoons frozen fruit juice concentrate (any flavor with no unwanted additives)

6 cups ice

"Real-food snow cones are basically just ice and juice!"

Strawberry Cheesecake Pops

Difficulty: Super easy
Prep time: 5 or 10 minutes
Freeze time: 4 to 5 hours
Makes nine or ten 2-ounce pops
Special tools needed: Blender,
  ice pop molds with sticks

GLUTEN-FREE
VEGETARIAN
NUT-FREE
FREEZER-FRIENDLY

1 cup plain yogurt

One 8-ounce package cream
cheese

1 cup frozen strawberries

⅓ cup pure maple syrup

1 teaspoon pure vanilla extract

These pops are a twist on classic strawberry cheesecake! And they're real-food approved, so go ahead and cool off with these on a hot summer day.

In the blender, puree all the ingredients until smooth. Dividing evenly, pour into the ice pop molds, insert a stick into the center of each, and freeze for 4 to 5 hours or overnight.

> **LISA'S TIP:** One my recipe testers said she froze this recipe in silicone muffin cups for smaller servings that didn't take as long to freeze, and they popped right out when ready. Love that idea!

Banana "Ice Cream"

If you've never tried this magical recipe, you're in for a real treat! The consistency of the bananas in this dish is identical to ice cream. And with pure ingredients like bananas and milk, you could technically even eat this one for breakfast if you wanted. (I speak from experience, ha ha!)

1. In a blender, combine the bananas with ¼ cup of the milk and any desired add-ins. Blend and keep adding small amounts of milk until the consistency resembles ice cream.

2. It's that easy! Serve with Homemade Magic Chocolate Shell, if desired.

> **LISA'S TIP:** It's best to freeze bananas with their peels off—otherwise you'll end up with a nearly impossible task! I also like to break mine into thirds or quarters for easy blending. So the next time you have some bananas that start to get a little too ripe, simply peel, break into pieces, and throw them in a big freezer container and freeze. You'll be well prepared next time you get a hankering for some wholesome "ice cream."

"My eleven-year-old loves to make this one all by herself!"

Difficulty: Super easy
Prep time: 5 to 10 minutes
Cook time: N/A
Makes 4 or 5 servings
Special tools needed: Blender

GLUTEN-FREE
DAIRY-FREE (IF A MILK ALTERNATIVE IS USED)
VEGETARIAN
NUT-FREE (IF PEANUT BUTTER ADD-IN IS NOT USED)
FREEZER-FRIENDLY

4 or 5 frozen bananas, the riper the better (see Tip)

½ cup milk (or less)

OPTIONAL ADD-INS: Peanut butter, chilled espresso, other frozen fruit—don't be afraid to get creative!

OPTIONAL TOPPING: Homemade Magic Chocolate Shell (page 287)

Orange Cream Bundt Cake

Difficulty: Medium
Prep time: 10 to 15 minutes
Cook time: 45 to 50 minutes (hands off)
Makes 10 to 12 servings
Special tools needed: 10-inch Bundt cake pan, electric mixer

VEGETARIAN
NUT-FREE
FREEZER-FRIENDLY

2 sticks (8 ounces) butter, at room temperature, plus more for greasing the pan

3 cups whole wheat flour

2 teaspoons baking powder

½ teaspoon salt

Grated zest and juice of 2 oranges (plus more zest for serving, if desired)

1½ cups pure maple syrup

4 eggs

¾ cup heavy cream

1 teaspoon pure vanilla extract

Small-Batch Whipped Cream (page 288), for serving

There's just something fun and special about a Bundt cake! And, even though the baking time in this recipe is a little longer than others in this book, this cake is really easy to make and so worth it in the end. Serve with homemade whipped cream and you'll have a crowd pleaser.

1. Preheat the oven to 350°F. Generously grease the Bundt pan with butter.

2. In a large bowl, whisk together the flour, baking powder, salt, and orange zest. Set aside.

3. In a large bowl, with the electric mixer, cream the butter on high speed. Mix in the syrup, eggs, cream, vanilla, and orange juice. Slowly add the flour mixture until well combined, scraping the sides with a rubber spatula as you go.

4. Pour the batter into the prepared Bundt pan and cook until a toothpick inserted halfway between the edge and center tube comes out clean, 45 to 50 minutes. Let cool for 5 or 10 minutes in the pan, then loosen the sides with a knife and turn out onto a cake plate so it's right side up. Let cool completely.

5. Slice and serve with whipped cream and garnished with orange zest, if desired.

CHAPTER 10

homemade staples

homemade staple recipes

Citrus Vinaigrette

When homemade salad dressing is this easy, there's no reason not to make it! Double the recipe and have it ready to go in the fridge before heading into a busy week.

Combine all the ingredients in the jar, screw on the lid, and shake vigorously until well combined (or use an immersion blender). Shake each time before use.

> **LISA'S TIP:** To keep honey from sticking to your measuring spoon, coat it with a little oil (or simply measure out the oil first if it's included in the recipe) and it will slide right out!

Difficulty: Super easy

Prep time: 5 minutes

Cook time: N/A

Makes about ⅓ cup

Special tools needed: Small jar with tight-fitting lid or immersion blender

GLUTEN-FREE
DAIRY-FREE
VEGETARIAN
NUT-FREE

3 tablespoons olive oil

2 tablespoons fresh lime juice

1 tablespoon honey

½ teaspoon salt

Fresh Ranch Dressing

Difficulty: Super easy
Prep time: Less than 15 minutes
Cook time: N/A
Makes a little more than 1 cup

GLUTEN-FREE
VEGETARIAN
NUT-FREE

½ cup buttermilk

½ cup sour cream

1 tablespoon chopped fresh parsley

1 tablespoon chopped fresh chives

1½ teaspoons fresh lemon juice

1 garlic clove, minced

⅛ teaspoon salt

Ground black pepper

Ranch dressing has always had a special place in my heart, especially when it's paired with crunchy Homemade Croutons (page 271). I don't even notice all the lettuce I'm consuming! This dressing is a great way to get little ones started on salad without any packets of highly processed powder.

In a bowl, whisk together the buttermilk and sour cream until smooth. Stir in the rest of the ingredients and serve over salad greens or store in the fridge for 2 to 3 days.

> **LISA'S TIP:** I used to think the dressing from those powdery packets of ranch seasoning mix tasted better than the store-bought bottle until one day, when I finally knew better, I checked the list of ingredients! Most of what's in there is definitely not real—yikes! Here's the list: maltodextrin, buttermilk, salt, monosodium glutamate, dried garlic, dried onion, lactic acid, calcium lactate, citric acid, spices, artificial flavor, xanthan gum, calcium stearate, carboxymethylcellulose, and guar gum.

Homemade Croutons

One thing is for certain—croutons are just all-around good stuff. So I felt I had to include this recipe, which is similar to one that first appeared with the Shortcut Caesar Salad in my first cookbook. And that's because homemade croutons are a fabulous addition to any type of salad, a wonderful garnish for soups, and even tasty plain as a snack!

1. Preheat the oven to 350°F.

2. On the large rimmed baking sheet, spread the bread cubes in a single layer. Evenly sprinkle with the Italian seasoning, garlic powder, and salt. Drizzle on the olive oil and toss to combine thoroughly (I like to use my hands or just toss all the ingredients in a large resealable bag). Spread them in one even layer on the baking sheet.

3. Bake, stirring once or twice, until golden brown, 14 to 16 minutes. The croutons will harden as they cool. For maximum crispiness, use right away, but you can store them for up to 1 day.

Difficulty: Easy
Prep time: 5 to 10 minutes
Cook time: About 15 minutes
Makes about 3 cups
Special tools needed: Large rimmed baking sheet

GLUTEN-FREE (IF GLUTEN-FREE BREAD IS USED)
DAIRY-FREE
VEGETARIAN
NUT-FREE

3 slices good-quality whole wheat bread, cut into 1-inch pieces (about 3 cups)

1 teaspoon Italian seasoning

½ teaspoon garlic powder

¼ teaspoon salt

2 tablespoons olive oil

Parmesan Crisps

Difficulty: Easy
Prep time: Less than 5 minutes
Cook time: Less than 5 minutes
Makes about 2 dozen 1-inch crisps
Special tools needed: Rimmed baking sheet and parchment paper

GLUTEN-FREE
VEGETARIAN
NUT-FREE

½ cup freshly grated Parmesan cheese (not the stuff in the green canister!)

This recipe is a super fun way to add some excitement back into salads, and it takes only minutes to make! Impress your next dinner guests with this simple and easy topping.

1. Preheat the broiler to high. Line a small rimmed baking sheet with parchment paper.

2. Sprinkle a very thin layer of the Parmesan in one big rectangle on the parchment paper. Place it in the center of the oven and keep a close eye on it. As soon as the outside edges start to turn brown and the middle is still light in color (2 to 3 minutes), remove from the oven. It will continue to cook and brown (and turn crispy) as it cools.

3. Let the cheese cool completely, then break it into roughly 1-inch pieces and serve.

> **LISA'S TIP:** This one tends to continue to cook once you remove it from the oven, and since overcooked Parmesan tastes bitter, if anything, take it out a little early (you can always stick it back in the oven for longer if necessary)! Also, I don't typically use parchment paper with the broiler, but since this one is in the oven for such a short period of time there are no issues.

Tzatziki Sauce

This Greek sauce, made with yogurt and cucumber, is incredibly versatile and simple to make. It is traditionally served with souvlaki and gyros, but it can also be used as a dip for veggies and whole wheat pretzels or as sauce to pour over chicken or serve with Lamb Burgers (page 215). It's also great thrown into a whole wheat wrap or pita with veggies or mixed in whole wheat couscous. The possibilities are endless!

Difficulty: Easy
Prep time: Less than 10 minutes
Cook time: N/A
Makes about 2 cups

GLUTEN-FREE
VEGETARIAN
NUT-FREE

Grate the cucumber (skin on) with a cheese grater and squeeze out and discard any excess liquid. Add it to a medium bowl with the rest of the ingredients and stir until well combined. Serve or store in the fridge for up to 5 days. The longer it sits, the better it is!

½ large cucumber

1½ cups plain yogurt (preferably whole-milk, but any type will work)

1 garlic clove, minced

1 tablespoon minced fresh dill or 1 teaspoon dried

1 tablespoon olive oil

1 tablespoon red wine vinegar

Hummus Without Tahini (Two Ways)

Difficulty: Super easy
Prep time: 10 minutes
Cook time: N/A
Makes 1¼ to 1½ cups
Special tools needed: Food processor

GLUTEN-FREE
DAIRY-FREE
VEGETARIAN
NUT-FREE
FREEZER-FRIENDLY

One 15-ounce can chickpeas, drained and rinsed

2½ tablespoons fresh lemon juice

2 tablespoons olive oil

1 garlic clove, minced

¼ teaspoon ground cumin

¼ teaspoon salt

OPTIONAL ADD-IN:

3 tablespoons chopped jarred red peppers (pimentos), with juice

Traditional hummus recipes—including the one on my blog—typically call for tahini (ground-up sesame seeds), but it's a rather pricey ingredient that I don't always have on hand. So I love this super quick and easy version, which also calls for canned chickpeas instead of dried, as an alternative!

In a food processor, combine all the ingredients and blend together. Add 1 to 2 tablespoons of water if necessary to make it smooth. Store in the refrigerator for 3 to 4 days or freeze. For Red Pepper Hummus, add the jarred roasted red peppers.

"Tahini is good stuff, but it can be pricey and I don't always have it on hand!"

Made-from-Scratch Simple Gravy

Whether it's for the holidays or just Sunday dinner, I beg you to please not use those highly processed store-bought packets of gravy mix to make your gravy! The ingredient list is full of refined additives (including "corn syrup solids"—no, thank you!) that you would not cook with at home. Plus it's SO super easy to make your own homemade gravy from scratch.

1. In a medium saucepan, melt the butter (or other fat) over medium-low heat. Carefully whisk in the flour, avoiding clumps. Cook, whisking, until the mixture darkens in color, 1 to 2 minutes. This step is called making a roux.

2. Whisk in the pan juices and/or broth and bring to a simmer. Cook, whisking occasionally, until the gravy reduces and thickens. Season with salt and pepper to taste and serve warm over meat or potatoes.

"Everything is better with gravy. I'm a big fan!"

Difficulty: Easy
Prep time: Less than 5 minutes
Cook time: 5 to 10 minutes
Makes about 1 cup

DAIRY-FREE (IF BUTTER IS NOT USED)
NUT-FREE
FREEZER-FRIENDLY

2 tablespoons butter (or fat separated from the roasting pan or slow cooker juices)

2 tablespoons whole wheat flour

1 cup strained roasting pan/slow cooker juices, fat separated and removed, and/or chicken broth (page 103)

Salt and ground black pepper

Slow Cooker Marinara Sauce

Difficulty: Super easy

Prep time: Less than 10 minutes

**Cook time: 5 to 6 hours on high
or 9 hours on low (hands off)**

Makes 5 or 6 servings

**Special tools needed:
6- or 7-quart slow cooker**

GLUTEN-FREE
DAIRY-FREE
VEGETARIAN
NUT-FREE
FREEZER-FRIENDLY

1 yellow onion, diced

2 large carrots, peeled and diced

5 garlic cloves, minced

One 28-ounce can crushed tomatoes

One 28-ounce can diced tomatoes (with juice)

1 tablespoon Italian seasoning

½ teaspoon salt

Big pinch of cayenne pepper

The key to a good homemade spaghetti sauce is letting it simmer for hours. And there's no better way to do that than in your slow cooker! We love the extra punch of veggies you get with the carrots in this one.

Combine all the ingredients in the slow cooker and stir to combine. Cover and cook on high for 5 to 6 hours or on low for 9 hours.

LISA'S TIP: If you're not a fan of chunky tomato sauces, then simply puree this when it's all done using an immersion or stand blender. That's how I prefer it!

"Your slow cooker is an easy way to let this sauce simmer for hours."

Pan-Fried Onion Topping

These tasty little onions are such a great way to top off burgers, soups, steaks, casseroles, and more, although we've been known to nibble on them just by themselves plenty of times!

1. Peel the onion and use a sharp knife to cut it into almost paper-thin slices. Break the slices apart into rings. Spread the flour on a plate and thoroughly coat each ring.

2. In a large sauté pan, melt the butter over medium heat. Shake the excess flour off the onions and add them to the pan, taking care not to overcrowd the pan (see Tip). Cook, stirring frequently, until golden brown all over, 3 to 4 minutes per side. Add more butter to the pan if it starts to look dry.

3. Transfer the onions to a plate lined with paper towels to drain. Season with salt to taste and cover with foil to keep warm until ready to serve.

> **LISA'S TIP:** Cook the onion in batches if necessary, wiping out any pan residue in between to prevent burning.

Difficulty: Easy
Prep time: 5 minutes
Cook time: 5 minutes
Makes about ½ cup

DAIRY-FREE (IF OLIVE OIL IS
 USED INSTEAD OF BUTTER)
VEGETARIAN
NUT-FREE

½ **large onion**

½ **cup whole wheat flour**

4 **tablespoons (½ stick) butter, plus more as needed**

Salt

DIY Oatmeal Packets

Difficulty: Super easy
Prep time: 5 minutes
Cook time: N/A
Makes 4 servings
**Special tools needed: 4 snack-
   size resealable bags or
   8-ounce jars**

GLUTEN-FREE (IF GLUTEN-FREE
   OATS ARE USED)
VEGETARIAN
NUT-FREE
DAIRY-FREE (IF MILK SUBSTITUTE
   IS USED)

2 cups rolled oats

**6 tablespoons raisins or other
dried fruit**

½ teaspoon ground cinnamon

Milk and honey, for serving

I know those store-bought instant oatmeal packets are convenient, but reading the ingredients list will have you thinking twice! Once I saw that the Quaker Strawberries and Cream flavor didn't even contain strawberries (they use dried apple pieces colored and flavored with artificial ingredients to resemble strawberries!), I was quickly done with those. So, as with any packaged food, it's best to buy plain and flavor it yourself with real-food ingredients!

1. To each plastic bag or jar, add ½ cup oats, 1½ tablespoons raisins, and ⅛ teaspoon cinnamon and seal tightly.

2. To make a serving of oatmeal, in a small saucepan, combine the contents of 1 bag with ⅔ cup milk and ½ teaspoon honey and heat for several minutes, until bubbling. Serve warm. (You can also do this in the microwave.)

> **LISA'S TIP:** If you're used to the highly processed packets of flavored oatmeal, this version may not taste as flavorful or sweet to you at first. Feel free to up the honey and cinnamon until your palate has had time to adjust.

Homemade Magic Chocolate Shell

My girls think Magic Shell chocolate sauce is super fun—and rightly so! It's hard to beat watching your chocolate sauce "magically" harden right before your eyes. And thanks to this homemade swap you can still have all that fun without any of the unwanted additives. Serve over any flavor ice cream—including banana (page 259).

1. In a small microwave-safe bowl, melt the coconut oil for 45 to 90 seconds in the microwave (depending upon how solid it is to start). Add the honey and cocoa powder and whisk until well combined. Pour over cold ice cream and wait about 30 seconds for it to completely (and magically) turn into a hard chocolate shell. Note: If the sauce hardens in the bowl, simply microwave it for 20 or 30 seconds to melt it again.

2. Store leftovers in the fridge for up to 1 week and reheat to melt as needed.

LISA'S TIP: You can of course pour this over store-bought ice cream, but I promise you—homemade is *way* better and worth the effort! Modern ice-cream makers are really easy to use and inexpensive. Give it a try and you'll never go back.

Difficulty: Super easy
Prep time: 5 minutes
Cook time: N/A
Makes about ⅓ cup
    (3 or 4 servings)

GLUTEN-FREE
DAIRY-FREE
VEGETARIAN
FREEZER-FRIENDLY

2 tablespoons coconut oil

2 tablespoons honey

4 teaspoons unsweetened cocoa powder (I prefer the "special dark" 100% cacao variety)

Small-Batch Whipped Cream

Difficulty: Super easy
Prep time: 5 minutes
Cook time: N/A
Makes 1 to 1¼ cups
Special tools needed:
 Medium jar (pint-size)
 with tight-fitting lid

GLUTEN-FREE
VEGETARIAN
NUT-FREE

½ cup heavy cream

1 tablespoon pure maple syrup
(optional; see Tip)

Whipped cream is nothing new for me . . . I have a recipe for it in my first cookbook and on my blog. And that's because we love it and are so glad it's "real food approved!" But let me rock your world with this new super easy and fun method for making whipped cream—I honestly don't even get my mixer out to make it anymore. And if you're entertaining, it's a fabulous way to put your guests to work (especially the little ones). I've even been known to put together two whipped cream jars and have a "boy team" and a "girl team" just to see who can whip their cream the fastest. All in good fun, of course!

Pour the cream and maple syrup (if using) into the jar and secure with the lid. Shake, shake, and shake until you no longer hear liquid hitting the sides and the product looks like whipped cream! This will take a few minutes. If you shake for too long you might end up with butter, which is great but not necessarily what you want. Have fun!

> **LISA'S TIP:** Whipped cream is traditionally sweetened, but it gets gobbled up at my house even if we don't add anything extra. If you do prefer yours a little on the sweeter side, I'd recommend adding up to 1 tablespoon maple syrup before getting started. You could also add a splash of pure vanilla extract as well for even more flavor.

"It doesn't get much easier than this!"

acknowledgments

"I am so grateful to so many!"

I could never have pulled this book together without the help of so many. Words cannot describe the amount of work that goes into writing a cookbook and how challenging it can be to find enough "spare time" in an already busy and full life to make it happen. After completing my first book I honestly wasn't sure if I could (or should) try to pull it off again or what my family would think about me taking on yet another big, stressful (yet fun and rewarding) project. So I was quite taken aback when I asked my sweet girls, Sydney and Sienna, if they thought Mommy should write another cookbook. I was certain they'd quickly say no and be happy to rid our lives of the distraction, but much to my surprise they both responded with a resounding yes. I was so shocked I said, "Why do you think I should write another book?"

And Sydney said, "Because it helps people and you are good at it." That girl is a keeper. So first and foremost, thank you to both of my precious daughters, for without your encouragement I would most definitely not be here.

To my husband, Jason, for your unconditional love and support as well as your willingness to be my sounding board any time of the day or night and for always agreeing to procure all those last-minute ingredients I seem to forget or suddenly decide I need! I hands down could not have done this without you and am one lucky girl to get to do life with you.

To my parents, for your unwavering love and support, as I said in the dedication. It's encouraging to know I always have you in my court, no matter what.

To my extended family and close friends, for sticking with me throughout this unexpected real-food journey. To Erin Rutherford, for helping me with all the clothes for the photo shoot, and so much more—including loaning me your cute kiddos, Riley and Brooks, for a few of the shots. I seriously could not have done it, and certainly not with such ease and efficiency, without you. To Valerie, Scott, Kate, and Sam Sappenfield for allowing me to subject you to hours of photos while pretending we weren't being subjected to hours of photos. For a family who doesn't love taking pictures, it meant the world to me for you to go to so much trouble to be a part of all the shenanigans. To Jenn Hennessy, for your continued willingness to be my "wingman" for TV appearances and for always having my back, no matter what. To Holly Chapman, for allowing me to rope you into all that unexpected recipe testing at the eleventh hour, and for keeping me company on last-minute trips to LA when necessary! To all my "blogging friends" (you know who you are!) for all your continued support.

To my agent, Meg Thompson, for continuing to believe in me even more than I believe in myself. I'm absolutely thrilled to have you on my side! To my editor extraordinaire, Cassie Jones, for making the editing process so incredibly smooth even on a new timeline. It definitely felt like we'd done this dance before! It never would have been so painless without you and the talented team at William Morrow, including Kara Zauberman, Anwesha Basu, Liate Stehlik, Lynn Grady, Tavia Kowalchuk, Rachel Meyers, Lucy Albanese, and Anna Brower.

To the talented people who made the lovely photos in this book what they are. Thank you to Lindsey Rose Johnson for the food photography and styling, Daniel and Candice Lanning with The Beautiful Mess for the lifestyle photography (memories my family will cherish), Cynthia Groseclose and her assistant, Rachel Feinberg, for food styling, and Carla Eustache with Style Perfect Events for prop styling. I enjoyed working with you all! Also to Anne Markey with Favor Me Events for connecting me with Dan and Candice, and to Jen Hansard and Jadah Sellner with Simple Green Smoothies for helping me connect with Lindsey. I'm lucky to have you in my life!

To Sammy and Melinda Koenigsberg, for allowing us with such grace to shoot photos at your lovely home, New Town Farms. To Matthews Farmers' Market (my favorite) and Whole Foods Market, for allowing us to shoot photos as well. As Sammy says, he always knows when I show up at the farmers market sans baseball cap and old T-shirt there will be a camera crew trailing not too far behind! To Kymm McLean with Who's the Fairest and Megan Clouse with Blushing, for making sure I looked presentable enough, even in the very early morning hours, without my baseball cap to hide behind. And to Planetbox, Yumbox, and UKonserve for sending all the fun lunch box supplies for us to use in the pictures.

To my incredibly loyal blogging team, Kiran Dodeja Smith, Shawn Keller, and Amy Taylor. This book would not have been possible without your constant behind-the-scenes support to keep the blog running smoothly.

Above all else, to the amazingly loyal readers of my blog and my first book. Your stories inspire me every day and are the reason I do what I do. Together, and with the help of others on this journey, real food is slowly becoming more mainstream, and my hope is that one day it will become the norm, as opposed to the exception, in our country. There's much more work to do and I'm thrilled to have your support.

RECIPE AND MEAL PLAN TESTERS

A huge thank-you to Meghan Alpern, for doing a bang-up job coordinating all my recipe testers (and even testing some herself), which took a huge weight off my shoulders. And of course to my lovely volunteer recipe testers!

I'm so grateful to have had a long list of recipe testers who willingly volunteered in the midst of their busy lives to test recipes and meal plans for me. It was especially meaningful when friends and family, from all walks of life, pitched in to help:

Ashley Bhargava, Jennifer Caulder, Jerry Collins, Jennifer Conway, Holly Chapman, Cori Davenport, Natalie Demby, Jennifer Dennis, Caroline Dubis, Yvonne Greenbaum, Emily Hess, Carrie Johnsen, Shawn Keller, Kathryn Kornegay, Jennifer Lindenberg, Andy and Stephanie Milford, Alison Milligan, Jamie Moore, Valerie Sappenfield, Kari Skinner, Kiran Dodeja Smith, and Cindy Wagner.

And a big thank-you to the many additional recipe testers who jumped in to help make this book what it is: Emily Allen, Tracy Andrews, Rachael Andrulonis, Kellie Bennett, Emily Bergner, Pamela Bitting, Maria Boyer, Heather Boyle, Katherine Bray, Amanda Brazee, Kristin Bullock-Herman, Tasha Burks, Shelly Burns, Rebekah Byrd, Dorothy Catella, Monica Chiarello, Carla Cobb, Amy Coe, Rose Coffey, Katie Compain, Christina Copenhaver, Heather Corin, Lisa Coughlin, Jason Cousino, Dawn Croissant, Kim Curtis, Lauren Cutrer, Kathy Damron, Alli Engelsma-Mosser, Jana Flanigan, Christina Fleming, Sandra Foraker, Alisa Friedman, Virginia Fritschler, Sarah Gaden, Sara Gaskill, Katie Gasper, Kaylee Glenn, Sandra Haddock, Lee Harrison, Melissa Holt, Gaby Hubbard, Angela Huffman, Brinn Johnson, Emily Jurlina, Amy Keaton, Stacie Kirchhoff, Kathryn Lansden, Jeana Lietz, Jodi MacKay, Donna MacKenzie, Noreen Marando, Michele Marchand, Caitlyn Mrazik, Eryn Myrick, Erin Neils, Jodi Nelson, Lisa Nemeth, Kim Norgren, Melinda Nusbaum, Kaci Oram, Diana Orr, Karen Paskow, Holly Reynolds, Brandi Robertson, Lauren Roger, Kelli Rowley, Pamela Rutledge, Elizabeth Sabogal, Julie Sallee, Ali Sheffield-Roberts, Lisa Shelby, JoAnn Shull, Michele (Shelly) Smitowski, Brandy Soapes, Heather Stefan, Sandy Strohman, Lindsey Swank Meili, Neva Sypniewski, Stephanie Taylor, Laura Thrash, Andrea Trowhill, Virginia Tzotzolas, Adela Vulpescu, Lori Whitesides, Constance Wilson, Kimberly Wirtz, BreAnna Wright, and Ashleigh Zincone.

notes and references

CHAPTER 1: SUPERMARKET STAPLES AND SECRETS

1. *Dirty Dozen List:* www.ewg.org/foodnews/dirty_dozen _list.php

2. *High-risk GMO crops:* www.nongmoproject.org/learn -more/what-is-gmo/

3. *The Center for Science in the Public Interest has:* www .cspinet.org/reports/chemcuisine.htm

4. *The vine-ripened variety:* awaytogarden.com/wp -content/uploads/2011/08/usda-tomato-ripeness-color -chart.gif

5. *So you end up with a tomato:* www.npr.org/2011/08/26/13 9972669/the-unsavory-story-of-industrially-grown -tomatoes

6. *Believe it or not, the government regulation:* www.cdc.gov /healthywater/swimming/pools/disinfection-team -chlorine-ph.html

7. *According to the Sugar Association:* www.sugar.org/other -sweeteners/artificial-sweeteners/

8. *And even when a label says "no trans fats":* www.fda.gov /Food/IngredientsPackagingLabeling/Labeling Nutrition/ucm079609.htm

9. *But it's actually "rare for someone":* www.organic consumers.org/news/older-americans-need-daily -protein-intake-keep-muscles-strong

Real Food References

BOOKS

Bittman, Mark. *Food Matters: A Guide to Conscious Eating.* New York: Simon & Schuster, 2009.
Pollan, Michael. *Food Rules: An Eater's Manual.* New York: Penguin Books, 2009.
Pollan, Michael. *In Defense of Food: An Eater's Manifesto.* New York: Penguin Books, 2008.

DOCUMENTARY FILMS

Fed Up, Katie Couric and Laurie David (producers), 2014.
Food, Inc., Robert Kenner (director), 2008.
In Defense of Food, Michael Schwarz (director), 2015.

WEBSITES AND BLOGS

100daysofrealfood.com
cspinet.org
eatwild.com
ewg.org
foodbabe.com
localharvest.org
nongmoproject.org
renfrowhardware.com (gardening tips)
simplegreensmoothies.com
superhealthykids.com
takepart.com
weelicious.com

universal conversion chart

Oven temperature equivalents

250°F	=	120°C
275°F	=	135°C
300°F	=	150°C
325°F	=	160°C
350°F	=	180°C
375°F	=	190°C
400°F	=	200°C
425°F	=	220°C
450°F	=	230°C
475°F	=	240°C
500°F	=	260°C

Measurement equivalents

Measurements should always be level unless directed otherwise.

$\frac{1}{8}$ teaspoon	=	0.5 mL				
$\frac{1}{4}$ teaspoon	=	1 mL				
$\frac{1}{2}$ teaspoon	=	2 mL				
1 teaspoon	=	5 mL				
1 tablespoon	=	3 teaspoons	=	$\frac{1}{2}$ fluid ounce	=	15 mL
2 tablespoons	=	$\frac{1}{8}$ cup	=	1 fluid ounce	=	30 mL
4 tablespoons	=	$\frac{1}{4}$ cup	=	2 fluid ounces	=	60 mL
$5\frac{1}{3}$ tablespoons	=	$\frac{1}{3}$ cup	=	3 fluid ounces	=	80 mL
8 tablespoons	=	$\frac{1}{2}$ cup	=	4 fluid ounces	=	120 mL
$10\frac{2}{3}$ tablespoons	=	$\frac{2}{3}$ cup	=	5 fluid ounces	=	160 mL
12 tablespoons	=	$\frac{3}{4}$ cup	=	6 fluid ounces	=	180 mL
16 tablespoons	=	1 cup	=	8 fluid ounces	=	240 mL

cookbook recipe chart by dietary need

Always double-check recipes/ingredients for potential allergens and review noted substitutions.

	GLUTEN-FREE	DAIRY-FREE	VEGETARIAN	PEANUT/TREE-NUT-FREE	FREEZER-FRIENDLY	PAGE NUMBER
Breakfast						
Avocado Toast	✓[1]	✓[2]	✓	✓		57
Simple Yogurt Crunch	✓		✓			58
Cinnamon Raisin Scones			✓	✓[3]	✓	61
Our Favorite Overnight Oats	✓[1]		✓	✓		62
Small-Batch Shortcut Granola	✓[1]	✓[4]	✓			65
Cheesy Hash Brown Casserole			✓	✓		66
Applesauce Oatmeal Pancakes			✓	✓	✓	69
California Omelet	✓		✓	✓		70
Sausage and Pepper Frittata	✓			✓		73
Crunchy French Toast Casserole	✓[1]		✓	✓	✓	74
Lunch						
Veggie Cream Cheese	✓		✓	✓		81
Sienna's Deviled Eggs	✓		✓	✓		83
Sour Cream and Onion Chicken Salad	✓			✓		85
Broccoli Cheese Soup			✓	✓	✓	87
Chicken Thai Pasta Salad	✓[1,8]	✓				89
Taco Salad	✓			✓		91

	GLUTEN-FREE	DAIRY-FREE	VEGETARIAN	PEANUT/TREE-NUT-FREE	FREEZER-FRIENDLY	PAGE NUMBER
Black Bean "Hummus" Tartine	✓[1]	✓	✓	✓		93
Caprese Pasta Salad	✓[1]		✓			95
Couscous and Tomato Salad			✓	✓		97
Crab-Stuffed Avocados	✓			✓		99
Tangy Pasta Salad	✓[1]		✓	✓		101
Tarragon Chicken Salad	✓					103

Salads

	GLUTEN-FREE	DAIRY-FREE	VEGETARIAN	PEANUT/TREE-NUT-FREE	FREEZER-FRIENDLY	PAGE NUMBER
Citrus Salad with Crispy Quinoa	✓	✓	✓	✓		108
Apple-Cheddar Side "Salad"	✓		✓	✓		111
Egg Salad with Bacon	✓			✓		112
Layered Jar Salad with White Beans	✓	✓[5]	✓	✓		115
Asian Rice Noodle Salad	✓[8]	✓	✓			116
Feta and Avocado Pasta Salad	✓[1]		✓	✓		119
Roasted Summer Veggie Salad	✓[1]		✓	✓		120
Cobb Salad	✓			✓		123
Simple Salad Mix	✓		✓			125

Sides

	GLUTEN-FREE	DAIRY-FREE	VEGETARIAN	PEANUT/TREE-NUT-FREE	FREEZER-FRIENDLY	PAGE NUMBER
Lemon and Apple Coleslaw (Without Mayo)	✓		✓	✓		131
Lime and Cilantro Coleslaw	✓		✓	✓		132
"Rice" Pilaf	✓[1]	✓[2]	✓[6]			135
Asparagus with Easy Dijon Sauce	✓		✓	✓		136
Cauliflower Nuggets			✓	✓		139
Brussels Sprouts with Bacon and Apple Juice	✓	✓		✓		140
Simple Green Beans with Almonds	✓[8]	✓	✓			143
Italian-Spiced Zucchini	✓	✓	✓	✓		144
The Easiest Homemade Applesauce—Ever!	✓	✓	✓	✓	✓	147
Simple Skillet Cornbread	✓		✓	✓	✓	148
Sydney's Roasted Potatoes	✓	✓	✓	✓		151

	GLUTEN-FREE	DAIRY-FREE	VEGETARIAN	PEANUT/TREE-NUT-FREE	FREEZER-FRIENDLY	PAGE NUMBER
Snacks and Appetizers						
Toasted Coconut "Chips"	✓	✓	✓			157
No-Bake Peanut Butter Oat Bars	✓[1]	✓	✓			158
Honeydew Green Smoothie	✓	✓	✓	✓	✓	161
Whole Wheat Lemon Raspberry Muffins			✓	✓	✓	162
Apple and Banana Kebabs with Peanut Butter Dip	✓	✓	✓			165
Copycat Cashew Cookie "LÄRABAR"	✓	✓	✓		✓	166
Corn Muffins			✓	✓	✓	169
Smoked Salmon Dip	✓[1]			✓		170
Easy Baked Falafel (Chickpea Cakes)	✓[1]	✓[7]	✓	✓	✓	172
Zucchini Stacks			✓	✓		175
Coconut Shrimp		✓				176
Moroccan Meatballs	✓[1]	✓[7]		✓	✓	178
Soups and Stews						
Quick Cauliflower Soup	✓	✓	✓[6]	✓[3]		185
Lentil and Sausage Stew	✓	✓		✓	✓	186
White Chicken Chili	✓			✓	✓	188
Kale, Sausage, and White Bean Soup	✓	✓		✓	✓	191
Slow Cooker Black Bean Soup	✓	✓[5]	✓	✓	✓	192
Slow Cooker Chicken Tortilla Soup	✓	✓		✓	✓	194
Easy Slow Cooker Steak Chili	✓	✓[5]		✓	✓	197
Gazpacho with Avocado and Crab	✓	✓		✓		199
Simple Dinners						
Black Bean Bowls	✓	✓[5]	✓	✓		205
Homemade Fish Sticks		✓[2,7]		✓	✓	206
Creamy Mac and Peas	✓[1]		✓	✓		209

	GLUTEN-FREE	DAIRY-FREE	VEGETARIAN	PEANUT/TREE-NUT-FREE	FREEZER-FRIENDLY	PAGE NUMBER
Crispy Pork with a Cracker Crust	✓[1]	✓[9]		✓		210
Veggie and Bean Burritos with Cilantro-Lime Crema	✓[1]		✓	✓	✓	212
Lamb Burgers	✓[1]	✓		✓	✓	215
Parmesan-Crusted Chicken	✓[1]			✓		217
Easy Fish Tacos with Pico de Gallo		✓[4]		✓		218
Roasted Summer Vegetable Pasta	✓[1]		✓	✓		220
Real-Food Sloppy Joes!	✓[1]	✓		✓	✓	223
Simple Salmon with Pinot Noir				✓		224
Arugula-Walnut Pesto Pasta with Zucchini	✓[1]		✓			227
Simple Roasted Pork Tenderloin	✓	✓		✓	✓	228
Weeknight Mushroom and Kale Pasta	✓[1]		✓	✓		231
Small-Batch Shrimp Boil	✓	✓		✓		232
Taco Stuffed Peppers	✓	✓[5]		✓	✓	235
Butternut Squash Pasta with Sage Brown Butter Sauce	✓[1]		✓	✓		236
Slow Cooker Shredded Pork and Bean Tacos	✓[1]	✓[5]		✓	✓	238
Weeknight Beef Bourguignon	✓	✓		✓	✓	241

Special Treats

	GLUTEN-FREE	DAIRY-FREE	VEGETARIAN	PEANUT/TREE-NUT-FREE	FREEZER-FRIENDLY	PAGE NUMBER
Cinnamon-Glazed Bananas	✓	✓[5]	✓	✓		247
Homemade Dark Chocolate Fudge Pops	✓		✓	✓	✓	248
Mint Chocolate Truffles	✓	✓	✓			251
Chocolate Banana Pops	✓	✓	✓	✓[9]	✓	252
Real-Food Snow Cones!	✓	✓	✓	✓		255
Strawberry Cheesecake Pops	✓		✓	✓	✓	256
Banana "Ice Cream"	✓	✓[10]	✓	✓[9]	✓	259
Orange Cream Bundt Cake			✓	✓	✓	260

	GLUTEN-FREE	DAIRY-FREE	VEGETARIAN	PEANUT/TREE-NUT-FREE	FREEZER-FRIENDLY	PAGE NUMBER
Homemade Staples						
Citrus Vinaigrette	✓	✓	✓	✓		267
Fresh Ranch Dressing	✓		✓	✓		268
Homemade Croutons	✓[1]	✓	✓	✓		271
Parmesan Crisps	✓		✓	✓		272
Tzatziki Sauce	✓		✓	✓		275
Hummus Without Tahini (Two Ways)	✓	✓	✓	✓	✓	276
Made-from-Scratch Simple Gravy		✓[2]		✓	✓	279
Slow Cooker Marinara Sauce	✓	✓	✓	✓	✓	280
Pan-Fried Onion Topping		✓[2]	✓	✓		283
DIY Oatmeal Packets	✓[1]	✓[10]	✓	✓		284
Homemade Magic Chocolate Shell	✓	✓	✓	✓[11]	✓	287
Small-Batch Whipped Cream	✓		✓	✓		288

NOTES

1. Use gluten-free bread/pitas/crackers/noodles/tortillas/breadcrumbs/oats as appropriate.
2. Substitute olive oil for the butter.
3. Omit the walnuts.
4. Substitute coconut oil for the butter.
5. Omit sour cream, butter, and/or cheese.
6. Substitute vegetable broth.
7. Omit the sauce.
8. Use gluten-free soy sauce.
9. Omit the peanut topping or peanut butter.
10. Substitute a milk alternative.
11. Most people who are allergic to tree nuts can safely eat coconut, but talk to your allergist before consuming.

index

Note: Page references in *italics* indicate photographs.